Poe Motion

Yorkshire
Edited by Annabel Cook

 Young**Writers**

First published in Great Britain in 2004 by:
Young Writers
Remus House
Coltsfoot Drive
Peterborough
PE2 9JX
Telephone: 01733 890066
Website: www.youngwriters.co.uk

SB ISBN 1 84460 373 3

Foreword

This year, the Young Writers' 'Poetry In Motion' competition proudly presents a showcase of the best poetic talent selected from over 40,000 up-and-coming writers nationwide.

Young Writers was established in 1991 to promote the reading and writing of poetry within schools and to the youth of today. Our books nurture and inspire confidence in the ability of young writers and provide a snapshot of poems written in schools and at home by budding poets of the future.

The thought effort, imagination and hard work put into each poem impressed us all and the task of selecting poems was a difficult but nevertheless enjoyable experience.

We hope you are as pleased as we are with the final selection and that you and your family continue to be entertained with *Poetry In Motion Yorkshire* for many years to come.

Contents

Lauren Spencer (12)   42
Rebecca Hebden (12)   42
Lauren Fox (11)   43
Kyle Shillito (12)   43
Shaunagh Conway (11)   44
Rachel Johnson (11)   44
Amy Cooper (11)   45
Sophie Steel (12)   45
Katie Newitt (12)   46
Robbee Kent (10)   46
Katie Cottrell (12)   47
Helen Sowden (13)   47
Philippa Wilson (12)   48
Josh Kirton (12)   49
Charlotte Wood (12)   49
Louise Boreham (13)   50
Charlie Lowe (13)   50
Lucy Worthington (12)   51
Grace Cooper (12)   51
Adam Illidge (12)   52
Alice Cressey (11)   52
Richard Stead (11)   53
Naomi Stevens (12)   53
Peter Hebden (14)   54
Persephone Jade Mucenieks (12)   55
Jamie Harber (13)   56
Charlotte Harrison (13)   57
Mark Walker (12)   57
Stephanie Hadjioannou (13)   58
Lee Rowson (14)   58
Luke Lynam (14)   59
Alexandra Robinson (13)   60
Daniel Bird (12)   60
Thomas Eaton (12)   61
Sophie Butterworth (12)   61
Rebecca Shaw (13)   62
Dale Sinnett (12)   62
Sam Brear (11)   63
Emma Thomas (11)   63
Katie Craig (11)   64
Charlotte Stevenson (14)   64
Rebecca Mallinder (13)   65

Leanne Hunter (12)	65
Leanne Swift (13)	66
Samantha Brook (12)	66
Stephanie Parsons (13)	67
Liam Duffy (12)	67
Terri-Anne Jones (11)	68
Gary Woodcock (12)	68
Ailsa Craig (13)	69
Kathryn Thorpe (13)	69
Beth Chesworth (13)	70
Tom Simpson (12)	70
Laura Marsh (13)	71
Lauren Russell (12)	71
Natalie Gill (13)	72
Daniel Kane (12)	72
Ruth Greaves (14)	73
Luke Barratt (12)	74
Matthew Tinsley (12)	74
Andrew Djokic (12)	75
Georgina Tate (12)	76
Lily l'Anson (12)	76
Joe Rudge (12)	77
Graham Wardle (12)	77
Cathryn Foster (12)	78
Victoria George (12)	78
Emma Naylor (12)	79
Michael Fox (12)	79
Joe Hammond (12)	80
Sam Railton (13)	80
Kate Benn (12)	81
Lauren Fillingham (13)	82
Hayley Siddall (14)	82
Leanne Crossland (13)	83
Laura Miles (13)	83
Shelly Walker (13)	84
Hannah Dawson (13)	84
Emma Hunter (13)	85
Sarah Magee (13)	85
Samantha Bryan (12)	86
Charlotte Bettison (13)	86
Nicola Foster (13)	87
Lauren Turner (13)	87

Elizabeth Evans (14)	88
Hayley Gaunt (13)	88
Joshua Cleland (13)	89
Matthew Bradley (13)	89
Ross Leith (13)	90
Peter Goult (14)	90
Chris Lewis (13)	91
Hannah Richardson (13)	91
Craig Mosley (11)	92
Louise Grogan (11)	92
Emma Marshall (13)	93
Danielle Jowett (13)	94
Catherine Millar (13)	95
Bradley Shepherd (12)	95
Rachel Crookes (13)	96
Kyle Turner (11)	96
Barney Horner (12)	97
Rebecca Gent (11)	97
Sam Brady (13)	98
Samantha Cleland (14)	98
Daniel Le Page (12)	99
Jennifer Ward (11)	99
Josh Wood (12)	100
Cheryl Chapman (12)	101
Hannah Blagg (12)	101
Michael Channer (12)	102
John Dobson (12)	103
Laura Turner (12)	104
Keri Cawthra (13)	104
Danielle Louise Hall (12)	105
Sarah Cowan (11)	105
Lucy Brown (12)	106
Sam Cook (12)	107
Daniel Jones (11)	107
Luke Duffy (13)	108
Victoria Connelly (11)	108
Gareth Ventom (13)	109
Lauren Jones (11)	109
Heather Cavill (12)	110
Ashleigh Jowett (11)	110
Simon Cudlip (14)	111
Jade Bannister (13)	111

Dixons City Technology College

Mohammed Waqas Khan (12)   180
Danielle Kenehan (13)   180

Pudsey Grangefield School
Nathan Dickinson (13)   181
Peter Mitchell (12)   181
Lewis Bowers (12)   182
Jenny Day (12)   182
Jennifer Whittam (12)   183
Daniel Styran (12)   184
Tom Yearby (12)   184
Amelia Milnes (13)   185
Laura Marshall (12)   185
Gareth Clough (13)   186
Chloë Orbell (12)   186
Jamie Delaney (12)   187
Paul Bond (12)   187
Jamie Carrington (12)   188
Amie Bennett (12)   189
Anilah Choudry (12)   190
Kim J Farrar (12)   190
Arron Richmond (12)   191
Lauren Stevens (12)   191
Esta Owen (12)   192
Catherine Foote (13)   192
Ayesha Siddiq (12)   193
Jenny Quarmby (12)   194
Bobbie Hancock (12)   194
Rupali Sharma (12)   195
Jake Town (13)   196
Fern Pullan (13)   197
Melissa Sahin (13)   197
Dawn Wood (13)   198
Holly Bland (13)   199
Hannah Rudge (12)   199
Hafsa Naz (13)   200
Laura Shearon (12)   200
Gemma Hughes (13)   201
Sam Benson (12)   201
Jake Wilson (13)   202
Melanie Knowles (13)   202

Rodillian School

The Poems

Looking Forward

Looking forward,
Upwards and onwards,
I was dreading my high school,
With the big and furious vending machines,
And the think the cool blond boys, please,
Man, I miss my school!

The science lessons,
You can blow things up,
And sometimes the food can make
You throw up!
Boy, I miss my school!

My poetry in motion, this is it,
How I'm getting through high school,
This is it,
Looking forward.

Brittany Lewis (12)
Buttershaw High School

Who Am I?

My first is in pocket and also in locket,
My second is in ice and also in dice.
My third is in truck but not in look,
My fourth is in Tom but not in Dom.
My fifth is in gate and also in late,
My last is in name but not in game.
I'm small and furry,
But very cute.

(A: Kitten.)

Natalie Maragh (12)
Buttershaw High School

Desire

Your eyes so full of sunshine
Your smile so full of joy
Your heart is warm with kindness
As you looked upon your boy

You are that match made in Heaven
Two angels side by side
Passion working overtime
As his hand begins to glide

You smile upon his features
And you both stand up to leave
To go to a place somewhere new
Which you have both foreseen

This desirable place awaits your call
And now your feet grow cold
Are you ready to lose it all
For that guy who's just called Paul?

You fall for his charms
And his work begins
While you lay there quiet and still
For now you've gone and lost it all
To a man who is big on gin.

Emma Milner (16)
Buttershaw High School

My Riddle

My first is in Jack but not in back.
My second is in sat but not men.
My third is in mean but not in den.
My fourth is in fish but not in pond.
My fifth is in eat but not in tap.

(A: Jamie.)

Jamie Duffy (11)
Buttershaw High School

Riddle's Riddle

My first is in right and also in wrong
My second is in smile but not in frown
My third is in duck but not in goose
My fourth is in dirt but not in soap
My fifth is in love but not in hate
My last is in innocent but not in guilty.

(A: Riddle.)

Luisa Hewson (12)
Buttershaw High School

Who Am I?

My first is in five but not in hive.
My second is in it and also in bit.
My third is in neat but not in beat.
My fourth is in pig and also in big.
My fifth is in ear and also in are.
My sixth is in or and also in red.
My last is in seat but not in eat.
Keep me warm in winter,

(A: Fingers.)

Paul Flatt (12)
Buttershaw High School

My Riddle

My first is in clown but not in town,
My second is in lock but not in knock,
My third is in pond but not in panda,
My fourth is in click but also in lick,
My last is in kidney but not in Sydney,
Sometimes when I'm set you can hear my beeping!

What am I?

(A: Clock.)

Ryan-Lee Haigh (11)
Buttershaw High School

My Riddle

My first is in care but not in dare,
My second is in help but not in yelp,
My third is in pay but not in grey,
My fourth is in pit and also in pip,
My last is in spray but not in day,
Sometimes you can sit on me.

What am I?

(A: Chair.)

Nathan Wadiun (11)
Buttershaw High School

What Am I?

My first is in crate but not in plate
My second is in rattle but not in battle
My third is in ice but not in race
My fourth is in space but not in pace
My fifth is in price but not in rice
My last is in sack but not in pack
Sometimes you hear me *crunch!*

(A: Crisps.)

Victoria Ferrand (12)
Buttershaw High School

What Am I?

My first is in rocks but not in cake,
My second is in flint but not in sail,
My third is in opal but not in chalk,
My fourth is in granite but not in tail,
My fifth is in jade, also in apple,
My skin can be rough and hard, I can be found anywhere
especially at the beach.

(A: Stone.)

Lucy Louise Ramsden (11)
Buttershaw High School

What Am I?

My first is in lick but not in suck,
My second is in come but not in go,
My third is in mine but not in yours,
My fourth is in pull and also in push,
My fifth is in open and not in shut,
My sixth isn't in buy but is in pay,
You get me out on a warm summer's day.

(A: Ice pop.)

Emma Stead (11)
Buttershaw High School

Who Am I?

My first is in late but not in date,
My second is in you but not in blue,
My third is in black but not in slack,
My fourth is in soup but not in loop,
My fifth is in tea but not in me,
My sixth is in skies but not in high,
My last is in rear and also in tear,
I like to swim in the sea,
My favourite game is 'bite those toes'.

(A: Lobster.)

Joanne Ramsden (11)
Buttershaw High School

A Liberating Thought

Where do you expect them to go when the bombs fall,
When a life is ruined in a shower of another man's hatred,
When a child's first vision is that of death of a mother?
No wonder they hate us.
No wonder they can't take a single breath without smelling
a rotting cocktail of dreams and flesh.
But we are the liberators.
We are the saviours.
We are the ones who enter a town and take away the power.
But yet again we are the ones who kill without breath,
without a single thought.

Tom Smith (15)
Carleton High School

A Few Short Seconds

It falls from the plane slowly
Heading for the ground
On its way to cause
Hatred and destruction.

For a few short seconds
The hope of the civilians
Is lost in the panic
Floating weightlessly in the sky
The bomb waits its turn.

Hitting the cold earth
Spilling dust and blood into the air
As the fires rage
For a few short seconds
All hope is lost.

Alex Ashton (16)
Carleton High School

Global Warming

'What is global warming, Sir? They said it on the news.'
'It's all about pollution, Tim, with people burning fossil fuels!'
'But what does it all mean, Sir? I do not understand.'
'Well it's with the sun and atmosphere, they're heating up the land!'
'How is that a bad thing, Sir? It seems quite fine to me.'
'The polar ice caps are melting, Tim, affecting all the sea!'
'What is it doing, Sir, doing to the sea?'
'The ocean level's rising, Tim, it'll flood both you and me!'

Dominic Priestley (13)
Carleton High School

The Curse Of Africa

The curse, the curse,
the poverty of Africa,
torn apart by war,
women told to sell themselves
children starved, ravaged by disease.

Six million people crippled by AIDS,
children born with a life of AIDS,
made to suffer their short, innocent lives,
suffering every day, no chance of a life,
passing on the curse, the curse.

The curse, the curse,
the epidemic threatens to destroy Africa,
weakness ravaging their frail bodies,
each day, a day closer to Heaven,
orphans hungry, slowly dying,
the curse, the curse of Africa.

Alex Dando (13)
Carleton High School

September 11th

September 11th, thousands died,
Where friends they wept and families cried,
The famous towers, down they fell,
The day was horror, anger and hell.

The morning began, same as before,
Workers oblivious, they entered Death's door,
The terrorist attack, came from up high,
Crashed into the towers, they knew they would die.

The day now is over, it's all in the past,
Those who had died, their memory will last,
September the 11th won't ever be forgot,
Rubble and wreckage, bodies left to rot.

Rachel Radtke (13)
Carleton High School

Twin Towers

A day New Yorkers will never forget,
Is one when their worst fear was met,
Not knowing that their loved ones may never come home,
Saying their last goodbyes on the telephone.

Bin Laden decided to bomb the towers at eleven,
Sadly sending thousands to Heaven,
Fathers, mothers and even friends too,
All died on that one day, because of who?

September the 11th was an act of violence,
What left New York in a long, lost silence,
Among the carnage and devastation,
A president came to unite his nation.

Rachel Hicks (13)
Carleton High School

Just Another Day

Another day is about to begin,
Trying hard to control the fear held within.
Keep out of his way is the best I can do,
As I cover the bruises, the lies seem untrue.

The anger and sickness I try hard to hide,
The days that I've hidden, the days that I've cried,
Excuses, excuses, life just isn't fair,
When I'm used as a punchbag does anyone care?

Laura Bennett (13)
Carleton High School

September 11th

Just another day like all the rest,
But for New York and its people it's one huge test,
Exchanging kisses and hugs goodbye,
Without them knowing that thousands will die.

People trapped in the 737,
Only one minute between them and Heaven,
Apart from the terrorists flying the plane,
Who would cause so much hurt and pain.

Inside the Twin Towers workers did look,
They knew in their hearts that they were all stuck,
As they ran for the door the plane crashed through,
People below were victims too.

The sound of the crash made an ear-splitting roar,
As the firefighters raced through the office door,
News reporters fled to the terrifying scene,
As New York stood together and worked as a team.

Survivors came stumbling out,
As people watched with great doubt,
The sky turned black with clouds of smoke,
As thick dust flew around, people did choke.

The towers swayed and fell to the ground,
As the terror spread all around,
Hope was washed out as we stood and stared
At the wreckage before us and the sky now bare.

Stephanie Oglesby (13)
Carleton High School

No!

No seeds to sew
No crops that grow
To help them on life's way
No rain that falls
No telephone calls
Day after day after day

No cure for ills
No care, no pills
Not enough help to seek
No birthday joys
No cards, no toys
Week after week after week

No food to eat
No Christmas treat
A life that's lived in fear
No clothes to wear
No one to care
Year after year after year

No water pure
No home secure
Always trouble and strife
No fun, no laughter
No happy ever after
Could you call this life?

Hannah Steel (13)
Carleton High School

I Am Trapped

I am trapped within the feeling
Nobody is there for me
My heart is empty and the space cannot be filled
But the scent of her is irresistible
I'll do anything to fill that space
I wonder if it hurt when she fell from Heaven
If my voice could be heard, I ask you God
To fill my heart with joy and to let the light of my life
The wonder, the star, may I dream and may time pass

Time is slow and the day is dull, I feel neglected
The love of my life doesn't love me back
She doesn't give back the emotion that is given to her
I lock myself away as if I don't exist, I'm trapped
Within the beauty of love and I dream my way through it
Hoping she would turn up in my dreams and heal what is broken.

Kieron Fitzgerald (11)
Carleton High School

Home!

After school, going home,
Finally finished, no need to moan.
Any homework for me to do,
Before I have time for any food.
After homework I can have fun,
Freedom at last for everyone.
Plan sleepovers for the weekend,
Phone friends for invites to send them.
Getting ready for bed,
No need to dread.
Watch some telly,
Don't be a nelly.
Peaceful times for me,
Listen to music on my knees.

Danielle Davis (13)
Crofton High School

My Little Sister!

My little sister,
She's got eyes like a dragon,
She says what she thinks,
She's a right little bad 'un!

She's got the laugh.
That is evil and cold,
I'm sick of telling her,
'Do what you're told!'

Although she is loud,
She's as sly as a fox,
I shout to my mum,
'Can we put her in a box?'

She strikes like a lion,
She nips like a crab,
Even though she is vicious,
I think she's fab!

Luke Waddington (12)
Crofton High School

Football

Ball's hard
Football is cool
Team is fast
School team is the best
The kit is black and blue
Playing games
Boots are gold
Floodlights sparkling
Cold and grey
Raining hard
Running like a cheetah
Music: DJ is wicked.

Ben Caines (12)
Crofton High School

My Nan's Rap!

Oh my nan she didn't like school
She had no friends as they called her a 'fool'
She never got the cane but she got the slipper
It hurt so much that it made her quiver.

As she got the slipper
People laughed as they watched her quiver
Only the head teacher was really nice
She hated the other teachers as they gave her lines.

Oh school started at 8.45
That's a bit early for us to arrive
Her school finished at 4.30
That's an hour longer than our school has been.

I feel sorry for my nan
But now she has a new life
I think I'll pay her back
By being really nice!

David Robson (11)
Crofton High School

My Brother

He's as cool as ice,
And really nice,
Strong as an ox,
Which can crush rocks.

Bald as a baby's bottom,
Which feels just like cotton,
Intelligent as a dolphin,
Who likes a bit of golfing.

Eyes like a hawk,
Likes a good walk,
So that's my story,
Of my funky brother!

Christoper Hill (11)
Crofton High School

My Sister

My sister's really cool
She always goes to school
Doesn't catch the bus
Never makes a fuss
Always in a mess
Sometimes likes a test
She's a really groovy chick
Who knows which clothes to pick.

My sister's really cool
But sometimes a fool
She really likes karate
And her hair's really ratty
My sister's really funky
Just like a monkey
She's very good at swimming
But doesn't like fishing.

My sister's really cool
Who doesn't like dirty tools
She's got a brainy mind
Who's always determined to find
When I am down
She never will frown,

So, that's my sister!

Matthew Swift (11)
Crofton High School

My Brother

He has bright blue eyes,
That sparkle like the sea,
He has light blond hair,
So he doesn't look like me.

My brother is like the Devil,
Evil at heart,
He loves teasing me,
And drives us apart.

He has a cute smile,
Which hides his sly soul,
He's quick to anger,
And is as black as coal.

Jamie Noble (11)
Crofton High School

My Little Bro

He smiles like the Grinch
He eats like a pig
He is as thin as a stick insect
He climbs like a monkey

He forces his burps out like a cat being sick
He forces laughs out like a hyena
He is accident prone like Mr Bean
And he is karate mad

I look at him sleeping then I think he's not that bad.

Joe Richardson (11)
Crofton High School

My Brother

Funny and cheerful,
Intelligent and wise,
His eyes remind me
Of misty blue skies.

Rosy-red cheeks,
Hair as bright as the sun,
My big brother
Always has lots of fun.

Mischievous and naughty,
But sometimes he can be kind,
He's the kind of brother
Who will always stay in your mind.

Amy Harrison (11)
Crofton High School

Friendship

Friendship is cool,
Friendship is fab,
But sometimes friendship makes me mad.
Friendship is wild,
Friendship is ace,
Friendship is like eating a strawberry lace.
Friendship is super,
Friendship is brill,
But sometimes it's like climbing a great big hill!

Lucy Hyett (11)
Crofton High School

My Dad

My dad
He is the best,
Funnier than all the rest.
Here are a few things about him.

As bold as a rock,
With lumps and bumps.
As tough as a lion,
But as soft as its mane.

His eyes like gems,
Sparkling in the sun.
As strong as steel
Like an automobile.

He stands out
Like black on white.
He always protects me,
That's nice to see.

He smiles like a Cheshire cat,
But that's enough of that,
All I need to know,
Is that he is the best dad in the world.

Tanya Vasey (12)
Crofton High School

Mates

My mates are crazy,
But they're not lazy.
My mates are clever,
And they can talk forever.
My mates are loud,
It makes me so proud.
My mates are always there,
I know they really care.
My mates are loyal,
To me they're royal.

Sophie Braim (11)
Crofton High School

Me And My Best Friends

Loyalty as though we're stuck together,
Bound with an elastic band.
We're ever so different but also alike,
Always there to lend a helping hand.

Our brown eyes are like chocolate buttons,
We natter on forever.
We like chocolate sweets and all things pink,
But mostly just being together.

Apart from spiders, we're afraid of nothing,
But if we're ever torn apart,
No one and nothing could ever mend
All our broken hearts.

But for now we stand strong,
Because we are together.
And we are blissful 'cos we know
We'll be best friends forever.

Emily Smith (11)
Crofton High School

My Sister

My sister is a real pain,
If anything's wrong I'm to blame.

She's vile, wicked and sometimes bad,
She's annoying and drives me mad.

Evil, mean, mischievous, nasty,
Rotten, naughty and quite ghastly.

She's snooty, snobbish, beastly, sly,
Stubborn, defiant, pretends to cry.

Connor Byers (11)
Crofton High School

My Brother

My brother is a couch potato,
Always saying, 'Do it later.'
My brother's brainy, bonkers and bad,
He drives me completely mad.

He's always eating sweet and sour,
Doesn't like the height of a huge tower,
My brother's got a cheeky grin,
But there's a monster lurking within.

My brother's fine,
So divine,
I don't like his style,
Needs to go shopping for a while.

My brother's bad, not at all good,
He's the worst in the neighbourhood.
I've been untrue, I'll tell no more lies,
He's the best in the world, I apologise.

Stephanie Mullins (11)
Crofton High School

My Big Bro

Our Gaz is such a slim Jim,
Although he has a cheesy grin

Annoying he may seem
But then again he is thirteen

He's always eating minging pizza
I call him a pizza gizza

His fringe is like a peacock
It could give you a nasty shock

He stomps his big feet everywhere
That's my big brother!

Kayleigh Ventom (11)
Crofton High School

Dragon The Hell's Beast

They wake in the early morn
Their lips flicker of flame
Their breath the gasoline
Their power is not for conquest
But they rule over some.

Skin as strong as mythril
It is a wondrous creation
Like layers and layers of bulletproof vests
They can take it all . . .
A bullet of wrath
A slash of an argument
An explosion of temper.

Their claws 12 inch unending
Stay clean through mud and rock
Their claws are a strange thing
They take more than a soldier on front line.

Their canine tooth is as sharp as a pinpoint
Pierce through flesh like a dagger
They progress to say white
Through a large and misty streak.

Their eyes are full of pain
They take in teenage anguish
They put up with it every day
How? Who knows.

So I think my mum's a dragon, she's been one all my life,
I think I shall stop this poem now,
She's coming, nooo . . .

Matthew Tingle (13)
Crofton High School

A View From A Window

As I glare out of the window straight in front of me is the lamp post
Flickering in the lonely, dark streets.
But then a squabbling sound hits my ears,
I look to the left of me and then a crowd of youngsters appear
From the corner of the street quarrelling over who won
The game of football.
Only something was different tonight.
What was it?
I sat and thought but then I realised,
The lonely girl with scraggy long hair that roams the street,
She wasn't there,
She was always there.
Every night at 9 o'clock.
I take a glance down the street,
There is an old man with a hunched back,
Stumbling along with his three-legged dog
Which has two front white paws.
I stare into the distance, in the black sky a small plane thunders by.
Then across the road Miss White comes dashing out of her house
To collect in the washing just as it starts to rain.
The dark streets suddenly go silent.
All you can hear is the rain crashing down
Onto the pavement.

Nicola Hinks (13)
Crofton High School

Lord Of The Rings

Lord Of The Rings is
one of my favourite things
There is Frodo, Sam
Gollum on their way to Mordor
Merry, Pippin and Treebeard going to Isengard
Legolas, Gimli and Aragorn chasing after Merry and Pippin
Saruman and Gandalf
Sauron and Treebeard
Frodo and Sam
Merry and Pippin
Gimli and Legolas
Aragorn and Gollum
Are the gang
The Shire
Isengard
Mordor
Rivendell
Gondor
Dwarf City, Moria
Fangorn Forest
Are the places in the films
There are Orcs
Urk-Hai
Cave trolls
Dwarves
Elves
Wizards
And Men!

Lindsay Child (12)
Crofton High School

The Sea Storm

The sea is bashing against the rocks
Whilst the fish try to run away
Water splashing up at people like they're enemies
Rocks crumbling like hard-boiled sweets
Boats crashing, scraping into rocks
As the sea pushes and barges the boats like hell
As lifeboats skim across the sea
To save people in the boats
Before the people suffer anymore and die
The sea starts to calm down a little
Then the sun comes out with seagulls
Then the lifeboats come back in for a little rest
People go back on the beach to play
When night-time falls people go home.

Garreth Hanley (13)
Crofton High School

Rose

In a rundown garden of rusty golden leaves
A lush, green, silky stalk
Yet prickly like a bed of nails to the touch
In the pouring rain it shines like diamonds in the desert sun
The petals as soft as a baby's chubby bum
People stop to see
The startling scarlet-red smooth petals
By its side weeds
Discoloured and going grey tangled like dreadlocks
All day they sway
I was a rose between two thorns.

Emma Brown (13)
Crofton High School

A Friend's Brother

Cute dreamer
Young reader
Little lover
Small cover
Funny smacker
Food attacker
Silly maker
Crying faker
Best kicker
Fast walker
Loud shouter
Great creator.

Stacey Tams (11)
Crofton High School

Aussie Kenning

Hearty sleeper
Strange speaker

Sexy singer
Kangaroo slinger

Architectural wonder
From down under

Horse eater
Special greeter.

Ian Martindale (11)
Crofton High School

My Baby Sister

My baby sister she is the best
She always shines above the rest,

With new people she is, so shy
But at the end she says 'bye-bye,'

She has the smile so cute and stunning
She is the baby who is so loving,

My baby sister is the best
She always shines above the rest,

It seems like she really cares
As she is like a teddy bear,

We all really love her so
She cheers us up when we are low,

My baby sister is the best
She always shines above the rest,

She always has a busy day
As all she does is play, play, play,

When she is asleep she is safe and sound
All tucked up in her dressing gown,

My baby sister is the best
She always shines above the rest.

Jessica Smith (11)
Crofton High School

My Big Sister

My big sister
She's a pain,
Sometimes I could
Give her the cane.

She has a laugh
That's evil and cold,
She never does
What she is told.

She has blonde hair
And says what she thinks,
She strikes like a lion
But really stinks.

My big sister
Her name is Stace,
Even though she's bad
I think she's ace.

Lee Crookes (11)
Crofton High School

Mum

My mum is soft-hearted,
She'd never hurt a soul,
She always works her heart out,
And she loves me like gold.

My mum is tall, like a giraffe,
Her hair is brown like a chestnut,
My mum's face is as bright as the moon,
And she will light up a room.

My mum is kind,
Her eyes are dark brown,
And her smile is welcoming,
She's the best mum in the world.

Daniel Lester (11)
Crofton High School

My Sister Leanne

Her hair is chestnut-brown with blonde streaks
When I wrap her presents she always freaks
She smiles like a clown
She's worse when she has a frown
She expects me to tidy her mess
Leanne will never wear a dress.

Leanne is funny
She could eat for England
She loves her honey
My sister loves Sean Paul
She never hears me when I call
Leanne blames me for the silliest things
My sister loves her gold diamond rings.

Chelsea Whitaker (11)
Crofton High School

Friends 'n' Family

Me and my friends have secrets never to be told
We all tell stories new and old
Me and my family we have such fun
They all take care of me, especially my dad and mum

Me and my friends love swapping gifts
We love going to town and going in the lifts
Me and my family who I love very much
We do things together then they feel touched

Me and my friends love to talk
Right up until we hear the owls hawk
Me and my family love to have a day out
I'm always happy even if I get 'nowt'.

Ashleigh Bateman (12)
Crofton High School

The Weather

Rain drizzled down
like it was coming from
big dripping taps in the sky
Umbrellas popped up
All over
It was a sea of colour
Everyone pulled up their hoods
And put on their hats and caps
It was dark and miserable
All the travellers
Pulled out their maps
To find the nearest shelter
It was a damp, dark, dismal day.

Jessica Fox (12)
Crofton High School

Sport

Floodlights shining
on the players
Pouring rain
getting wetter
Freezing cold
when you're waiting
Working together
for the ball
so you can score a goal
People try to keep dry
but they're mostly getting wet
Sport is what we like to play
we play football every day.

Zack Wynn (12)
Crofton High School

Winter Poem

Cold is winter,
White is winter.
Happiness means winter,
Stockings are winter.

Ice is winter,
Wet is winter.
Carols mean winter,
Wellies are winter.

Snow is winter,
Santa is winter.
No leaves mean winter,
Runny noses are winter.

Chilly is winter,
Hot chocolate is winter.
Christmas means winter,
Happy faces are winter.

Winter is a time to celebrate,
Enjoy the cold and frosty months.
So wrap up warm,
And don't forget goosebumps!

Nichola Radecki (12)
Crofton High School

The Big Day

The big day is coming up
Arsenal challenge for the cup
Man U play on their own turf
They know what the victory's worth

Cheering, screaming, the crowd go wild
The game of the season isn't mild
The Gunners are beaten 2-0
What a game, what a thrill.

Josh Wynn (13)
Crofton High School

Summer

People sweating
Squidging of suncream
Ice cream melting
Cold drinks gushing
People in coloured bikinis
People lying on the golden sand
People tying hair back with rubber bands

Shining sun glistening on the sea
People having picnics for their tea
Children building sandcastles
People playing in the clear blue sea.

Vicky Flanagan (12)
Crofton High School

My Grandad

My grandad is kind,
With a personality that shines,
He is friendly and funny,
And really cuddly,
Almost like a stuffed teddy bear,
But still he's always there to care,
He has a dark brown tan,
And he is a very clever man,
He is so clever he should work in a lab,
That's my grandad, he is fab!

Sarah Mills (12)
Crofton High School

My Favourite Place

The beautiful, colourful, fantastical lights
The lovely sound of the roaring seagulls
The strong smell of colourful candyfloss
The strong smell of the fish and chips, fantastical smell in the air
The grey, cold sea roars onto the golden beach
The rumbling sound of the colourful trams
Trudging along the track
The arcade of brightly coloured lights
People chucking in coins waiting to win a fortune
The children playing on the golden beach
I feel happy
All these things are what I love about Blackpool.

Caroline Sykes (15)
Crofton High School

Country Dream

River trickling down behind you
Bluebells hiding in hedgerows
Church bells ringing in the distance
The sound of no motorcars
Kids playing in the park
The sky as deep as the deepest ocean
Sheep grazing in the field above
Oh no clouds come, rain appears
Fade into darkness then you wake up from a deep sleep.

Benjamin Wilby (15)
Crofton High School

Break Time

The bell rings
And break begins
Pupils pouring into the playground
Splashing through puddles
Gangs of people huddled together
A football booted across the yard
Trees swaying
Rain racing down the gutters
Into the flooded drains
Girls screaming
Don't want to get their hair wet
Boys shouting
Teachers moaning
Get undercover
A small child
Crying in the corner
The bullies run away
Bins overflowing
Litter blowing
Smokers behind a bush
Teachers catch them in the act
The bell rings
And lessons begin.

Gareth Mears (16)
Crofton High School

Jamie Lee

Eyes shining like little stars
Hair bouncing with the wind
Pink dresses flying into the trolley
One with a little purple brolly

On sunny days we go to the beach
Digging, building lots of sandcastles
Choosing an ice cream after tea
Chocolate for her, strawberry for me

My sister is just really fun
Giggling, singing in the pool
Time for bed, up you go
See you in the morning

Leave me alone!

Sarah Shackleton (12)
Crofton High School

Football

Crunching tackles flying in
Broken legs
And arguing
People shouting
People fighting
Football studs
And all the sliding
Yellow cards for bad offence
People shout, 'It could be a red,
Come on Ref, use your head'
At the end of the game it's all a loss
All the players are feeling off
But still can't wait until the next kick-off
'We'll turn it around,' says the boss.

Liam Maw (15)
Crofton High School

The Mysterious Night

It was a cold, windy, blustery night,
Creepy trees staring with nasty faces,
Shadows gradually enlarging themselves,
Television screens blurring,
Hall lights twitching,
Me sitting on the chair,
All alone.

The big black doors slamming,
Doors opening with the strong, powerful wind,
Taking my quilt away.
But me in the chair,
Sitting on my own,
All alone.

Ornaments smashing,
Glass bottles breaking,
Eventually I wake up,
With the silent morning,
The sun is shining,
What a beautiful day.

Stacey Horsfall (13)
Crofton High School

Rain

Rain is boring,
Rain means house,
Rain means inside,
Rain is wetness,
Rain is slippery,
Rain is dark clouds,
Rain is empty,
Rain is a drip,
Rain's usually winter,
But leaves a fresh smell.

Chris Swaine (13)
Crofton High School

My Prayer For Peace

Peace would be so wonderful,
Life would be so colourful.
No more war,
Let it exist no more.

Peace would be so wonderful,
Life would be so colourful.
There would be no hate,
Don't let us leave it too late!

Peace would be so wonderful,
Life would be so colourful.
People killing, innocent people dying,
The news tells us people are crying.

Peace would be so wonderful,
Life would be so colourful.
So stop and think,
Try to make lives peaceful.

Charlotte Halstead (13)
Crofton High School

The Game Of Football

The smell of food, the smell of smoke
My mate next to me is drinking Coke
The taste of victory, the taste of fire
My favourite footballer is Kieran Dyer
When we are losing I'm gutted, I go boozing
But when we draw it is such a bore.

Luke Capstick (12)
Crofton High School

Autumn

It's the first day of autumn,
I step out of the door,
Onto all the frosty grass
And into a cold morning.

It's the second day of autumn,
The leaves have changed
And fallen to the floor,
So the trees are bare.

It's the third day of autumn,
Mornings are frosty,
Conkers galore,
Let's go and get some more.

It's the fourth day of autumn,
Dark nights have come,
Hallowe'en is here,
Tonight we go to scare.

It's the fifth day of autumn,
There's smoke in the air,
Chestnuts for tea,
Toasted on a bonfire.

Laura O'Donnell (13)
Crofton High School

Autumn Poem

A utumn is here again,
U nder trees and everywhere,
T here you see a shell of spikes,
U nder the big horse chestnut tree,
M illions are there on the floor for you to pick them up,
N ow we wait for winter to come but we say farewell to autumn!

Scot Hemingway (12)
Crofton High School

Brothers And Sisters

Brothers are noisy,
Brothers are dozy,
Brothers are annoying,
Brothers are stupid.

Sisters are friendly,
Sisters share things,
Sisters are nosy,
But that doesn't mean a thing.

Brothers and sisters
Are different in many ways,
But we will always love them
Whoever they are.

Aimee Barlow (13)
Crofton High School

Our House

In our house it's quite a fright,
The screaming and shouting is quite a sight.
My brother's playing with his gun,
Shooting people and having fun.
My dad's reading his paper,
And my mum's trying to fix the coffee maker.
Then there's me, all quiet, safe and sound,
Just cuddling my scruffy hound.
In our house there's not a minute's peace,
They really are louder than quacking geese.
In our house it's quite a fright,
The screaming and shouting is a sight.

Lauren Harrison (14)
Crofton High School

My Dog Poem

My dog is fun
My dog is great
My dog is happy
My dog is loving
My dog is brill
My dog is mine

My dog is soft
My dog is Molly
My dog is sweet
My dog is hot
My dog loves me
My dog has me
My dog is mine

My dog is handy
My dog is helpful
My dog is small
My dog is sleepy
My dog is messy
My dog is three months old
My dog is mine.

Jaysie Davies (13)
Crofton High School

Summer Poem

S ummer is here again
U nder the trees children sneeze
M unching away at their cold ice cream
M any have different flavours
E veryone gets brain freeze
R ound the corner autumn waits until summer disintegrates.

Tom Yates (12)
Crofton High School

Football

Riots
Excitement
Player nerves
A jam-packed stadium
The game will soon begin
The roar from the crowd
Like a lion
The smell of fast food
Cigarette smoke drifts across the north stand
The ball boys are excited
The teams are ready
The roar gets louder
The teams come out
The fans are ready
And chanting songs
United win
The game is over.

Luke Lythgoe (14)
Crofton High School

BMXing Rap

Hey everybody let's write a rap
Let's put skate parks on the map
We'll go to the parks
And make some sparks
We'll wax the rails
And make some trails
Your tyres pop
And you blow your top
You have to walk home
With a broken bone
You walk down the paths
Doing your maths
Hey everybody let's write a rap
Let's put skate parks on the map.

Jamie Markey (13)
Crofton High School

Terrible Teachers

Teachers tell us what to do
The real good times are far and few
We're so bored in our mind
They never get the boredom sign
We get blamed for all the trouble
Then we get homework by the double

Detention slips are always sent
But when I had mine I never went
Teachers catch us out when we chat
I bet they think I'm a little brat
Report books are flying everywhere
It really is one big scare

My legs are trembling, I'm in a state
Because my English homework's late
She looks at me with an evil stare
'Detention at twelve,' I better be there
I went to her room and all I could see
Was my head of year waiting for me!

Jody Wray (12)
Crofton High School

Fire

Fire, fire burning bright
Licking the walls on a cold, misty night
Like a hungry tiger searching for prey
It spreads around in a fierce kind of way.

Fire, fire burning bright
It lights up the house on a winter's night
Like a big swarm of bees buzzing around
It scorches my feet that stand on the ground.

Fire, fire burning bright
Its breath is warm, its fingers are alight
It burns all around me and crouches down
It dies in peace and flickers to the ground.

Natalie Outhwaite (12)
Crofton High School

Peace

Peace is goodness
It could exist on this earth
Peace is happiness
Like a new birth

I dream at night
Of a place
Where we do not fight
With a happy face

Trees were tall
With giant leaves
Instead of a mall
With its thieves

Hopefully the world
Will change into this place
While I'm in my bed all curled up
With a sleepy face.

Lauren Spencer (12)
Crofton High School

Ball

Window breaker,
Happiness maker,

Good kicker,
Hard hitter,

Scary bowler,
Fast roller,

Goal scorer,
Not a borer,

High bouncer,
Big pouncer,

Bail shaker,
Wicket taker.

Rebecca Hebden (12)
Crofton High School

My Mystery Object

Face stretcher,
Come on and fetch her.

Fast whizzer,
Couldn't miss her.

Fashion traveller,
Metal dazzler.

Two-wheel rider,
Standing driver.

Pavement glider,
Swift as a spider.

Skateboards are wider,
Much more than a fiver.

Bike hater,
Play with you later!

Lauren Fox (11)
Crofton High School

Motorbikes

M ad bikes growling in the dark
O ver the limit they speed
T rying to go faster
O ut-doing the police
R acing through villages
B reaking the sound barrier
I tching to ignite
K icking up a fight
E xciting, lion roaring
S hivering like a dog.

Kyle Shillito (12)
Crofton High School

My Dolphin Friend

The water was cold,
Neck and neck we were.
Thrashing about, pulling forward,
I glanced across and caught his eye.
He returned my look,
Gave me a smile that melts.
Those teeth so white,
We slowed then stopped,
He turned with ease,
And snuggled in close.
I held him tight,
My hand it smoothed,
His so soft head.
I closed my eyes and wished,
I didn't want this moment to pass,
When all too soon,
The time came,
With a leap in the air,
And a glide so slow,
My dolphin friend,
    Had to go.

Shaunagh Conway (11)
Crofton High School

Nature

The trees swaying as the wind whistles,
Reaching out their bony fingers to the beaming rays of sunshine.
Flowers opening out of their buds, creating a new life.
The rivers flowing, their dancing ripples shine
And glitz as the sun smiles down at them.
The sound of birds sweetly singing while swaying
                        smoothly in the blue sky,
Amazing the people below.
But sunset soon comes and the children lie in bed,
Waiting to wake up to find a new life of a new day.

Rachel Johnson (11)
Crofton High School

My Brother

Footballer
Getting taller
Good attacker
Weird waker
Silly slacker
Crazy maker
ICT breaker
TV watcher
Xbox player
DVD buyer
Daft word sayer
McDonald's eater.

Amy Cooper (11)
Crofton High School

Earth

As the bright stars lurk above,
Its face spins around
And stares into space,
Searching for its distant friends.

Surrounded by beady eyes,
Constantly moving
Gliding and whirling,
On a silent winter's night.

The night is cold and silent,
Not a sound is made.
Its face still turning,
Lights ever switching on and off.

Sophie Steel (12)
Crofton High School

Friends

Every time I'm down,
My friends are always around,
Every time I'm feeling blue,
They always say, 'What's up with you?'
They always make me smile,
If only for a while.
They give me a shoulder to cry on,
A good friend I can always rely on.
Every day we're having fun,
Laughing, giggling in the sun.
I care about all my friends,
I love it when we make our dens.
I hate it when we all fall out,
I just want to scream and shout.
Our secrets we tell and share,
When we are all playing dares.
Never let your friend down,
Then they will always be around.

Katie Newitt (12)
Crofton High School

The TV

When I turned on my TV it buzzed
And went black and white like a zebra
Then its smooth face let out a blinding light
And it stared at me fiercely
It was like the TV had some eyes
Like a bloodthirsty T-rex.

It mumbled and made a weird sound
And it was really like it was alive
It was like it was talking to me
Then it first went off and it buzzed again
Like a TV coming out of its sockets.

Robbee Kent (10)
Crofton High School

Kaleidoscope

White is a colour that everyone loves
It reminds you of the clouds up above
White is milk
As soft as silk
White is snow falling to the ground
Snowflakes fall but they don't make a sound

Pink is a colour that everyone adores
Every time you wear it you get an applause
Pink is roses
As bright as fairy lights
In the dark nights.

Blue is sky
Blue is sea
Every time you see it
You fill up with glee
This is the colour that represents me.

Katie Cottrell (12)
Crofton High School

A Winter's Day

The heavy, dark sky
The long lasting rain
The sound of the wind
The silence of the day

I run along
Down it hits
Splashing through my cheeks
The arms of the trees
Pointing to me

The birds
Fly away
And everything is still . . .

   I'm alone.

Helen Sowden (13)
Crofton High School

Winter Days

Day 1

It's winter again
It'll soon be Christmas
Lots of cold nights
Wrapped up in your home
With your fire on.

Day 14

I open my door and rush outside
The snow is dripping down
And landing on my nose
The icicles hanging from tree to tree
It's so exciting
It's happening to me.

Day 20

I open my door and rush outside
The snow is still there
Trees standing bare
I can't wait till Christmas.

Day 25

Hooray, hooray! It's Christmas Day
I look outside, the children play
It's like I've won the lottery
Fairy lights twinkling,
It's like winter's not here
It's nearly the end of our special winter year.

Philippa Wilson (12)
Crofton High School

Lesson

The school bell rings as the teacher walks in
Ties up, shirts in, chewing gum in the bin
Stop your talking, get into your chairs
Silence please in your pairs.

The school bell rings as PE begins
Roaring, snoring, these teachers are boring
On the pitch with the wet ball
Slipping, sliding, it's like climbing a wall.

The school bell rings for the end of the day
As all the children run to the bay
Buses earning, as children spend
Till tomorrow you just wait.

Josh Kirton (12)
Crofton High School

Winter's Here

Winter is here
It's that time of year
When families reunite
Into the night

We're having a party
We all start to bop
Mum, Dad and even Gran
Then the bottle goes *pop*

Grandad reaches for the Scotch
The time goes so quick
Everyone gone, now the house is dead.

Charlotte Wood (12)
Crofton High School

The Christmas Holiday Feeling

The Christmas tree
Shimmers in the dark
The snow drifts gently
In the park.

Mince pies are out
On Christmas Eve
In Santa Claus
They all believe.

Presents sit wrapped
Until the morning
The sun has woken
Children are yawning.

Presents are opened
And spirits are high
Mum got drunk
And fell in the pie!

January's here
It's gone way too fast
At least Christmas
Went off with a *blast!*

Louise Boreham (13)
Crofton High School

Remember

Life without you would be hell on earth,
So I'd just like to say for what it's worth,
You're my heart, my home, my health and soul,
You are so vibrant, bright and bold.
It's too late now, all hell is unleashed,
Because I'm still stood and you're deceased.
Stood on the snow that covers your grave,
Laying my flowers it isn't so brave.
But I'll remember you now the only way I know,
Of how much you always loved me so.

Charlie Lowe (13)
Crofton High School

Winter Fun

Snow's everywhere
The trees are bare
It's winter
It's winter.

Snowball fights
The cold frost bites
It's winter
It's winter.

Carol-singers at my door
Cold snow drips to the floor
It's winter
It's winter.

Christmas is near
The sky is clear
It's winter
It's winter.

But now it's time for summer sun
We'll wait again for winter fun!

Lucy Worthington (12)
Crofton High School

Fireworks

F irework display is about to start
I n the centre of the park
R aging children jump to see
E normous bangs as buzzy as a bee
W *hoosh, bang,* everyone smiles
O ver here you can see for miles
R oaring, racing rockets rage
K aleidoscope, colourful sparkles I see
S pecial night has soon gone, just wait till next year
  it'll go up in a bang.

Grace Cooper (12)
Crofton High School

Fear

I look through my window and I am scared
I am scared of the darkness which haunts me
Through the day and through the night
No light, just darkness

I look through my window and I am scared
I am scared of the silence which is everywhere
I, a deserted warehouse in the middle of nowhere

I open my curtains and the darkness has gone
I am not scared of the light which is everywhere
There is no darkness, just light

I open my blinds and the darkness has gone
The silence has gone and I hear children playing
Now I can sit in my chair and not be alone
Because the fear has gone.

Adam Illidge (12)
Crofton High School

Horse Rider

Happy hunter, jockey jumper
Running racer, 1st place taker
Horse rider, steady strider
Carrot cruncher, crazy lunger
Muddy hoofer, mad mover
Galloping whizzer, he's all in a dither
If in danger, he is really major
Stable shutter, wacky nutter.

Shoe clacker, water splatter
Amazing eater, easy treater
Naughty flipper, hurtful kicker
Teeth ripper, skin chipper
Daft prancer, silly dancer
Onward strider, pull back tighter
Frightful canterer, soft lander,
Heavy trampler, onward canterer.

Alice Cressey (11)
Crofton High School

The Wood

As I entered its woody mouth,
It blocked the light instantly,
Like I should never have come.
It was whispering to me
Its voice was colder than stone.

As I approached the vines
They leapt out
And grabbed me like a tiger
Hunting its prey,
I scrambled away,
There was a sudden shudder up my spine.

The roots of the trees
Were like old women's fingers,
The branches looked like withered corpses,
I would never escape
This death-hold.

Richard Stead (11)
Crofton High School

Winter

I open my eyes to see clear icicles
hanging from my window
I jump out of my bed
But I bang my head on the wall.

I crawl to the window
Pull myself up to see
The white snowflakes drifting
Down my windowpane.

I just can't wait to go out
I run down the stairs
Out of the back door
Then fall on the floor with a thump
I try to pull myself up
But I fall with a bump.

Naomi Stevens (12)
Crofton High School

Dealing With Boredom

Thursday afternoon, twenty past one,
History again, really fun!
That was sarcasm, by the way,
History is the slowest lesson of the day.
Learning about some forgotten war,
I think history was designed to bore.
'Write an essay on World War II,
And you fail, it's detention for you.'
As the message sinks in, a groan floods around,
Teacher screams, 'Silence, don't make a sound!'
Like a great bag of wind he sets off round the room,
Sniffing out trouble and condemning it to doom.
So I'm left alone at my table,
My mind tries to think but I'm not able.
This is so dull, I'm going to cry,
Before the end I think I could die.
I'm suddenly aware that it's twenty past three,
Sat with my blank page staring up at me.
Teacher is there, staring down,
This isn't good, he's wearing a frown.
He begins to rant, then starts to rave,
To be anywhere but here is what I crave.
Then I decide I've had enough,
I'm not taking any more of this punishing stuff.
As I push him back, there's a gasping of breath,
As he shatters through the window and falls to his death.
Top floor to bottom in two seconds flat,
And hits the ground with a resounding splat!
I suppose I should run, I should flee,
Ah well . . . at least no homework for me!

Peter Hebden (14)
Crofton High School

Why?

Crofton feels on fire as her lips, burning bright, burn menacing holes in the golden crops that are keeping people living.
As she laughs at the pain she's causing.

Then comes the lightning as she stares angrily at the innocent people like ants to her greatness and ugly weaklings compared to her pale beauty and evil power. She spits hailstones in disgust.
And laughs at weaklings below her.

Then suddenly, Crofton becomes invisible to all around as she lifts her thick veil of fog, thronging the air. The humans try to fight back with cosy hats and gloves like shields against her powerful wrath but she still fights on like a warrior. The pretty petals on once blooming flowers (her heart) droop and the beautiful colour fades from the pain of her heart.
But she still laughs at the deaths she's causing.

Then comes the thunder from the once blue skies, her heart breaking into shatters as someone chops down a growing tree below, drops litter which bounces off the ground from the vibrations of the thunder or kills a poor, helpless animal for the sake of looking good to friends.

She now sheds a tear across the whole world as people are brutally murdering her every day, slowly and painfully. They don't care about the pain they're causing. They don't think about the innocent animals, like her children, every day dieing for their evil pleasure and the way they're killing the once lush lands built up by her own hands, just for them. Why should they have the pleasure and privilege of life on her earth and the right to murder her animals?
Why should Mother Nature be slowly, brutally murdered
for our evil pleasure?
Why?
Why?
Why?

Persephone Jade Mucenieks (12)
Crofton High School

A Football Game

As the two teams walk out onto the pitch,
They're like an army going into battle.
No fear on their anxious faces,
They can't afford to lose.
It's the biggest match of the season.
The whistle blows, they kick-off,
Ooh, it goes out off the post.
The crowd start to encourage their team,
'Come on,' shouts a man like a raging bull.
Bang, a defender knocks him to kingdom come.
Penalty, the player steps back like a mouse cornered by a cat.
He smacks it but what a save by the keeper.
The half-time whistle blows.
The score is still 0-0.
One manager blows a fuse and he turns into a raging bull,
As he destroys everything in his path.
Thankfully the bell rings for the second half.
they restart their gruelling derby of a match.
This ain't no match, it's a death chamber.
Crunching frantic tackles flying in from everywhere.
It's like a volcano erupting, destructing, attacking a house.
There's a minute left and the ref gives a pen.
It was surely a dive.
The other players show the ref what they think
The ref escapes the chants and blows,
With his heart going ten to the dozen, he smacks it.
Goal 1-0, and the final whistle blows.
He is piled by his teammates as they walk in the tunnel
'1-0,' roar the fans.

Jamie Harber (13)
Crofton High School

View From A Window

Straight ahead of me I see trees filled with crispy brown leaves
that sway in the wind
On the left I see rooftops of my street
And very far away I see hills and fields
Patches of yellow and green
Something is different today
The couple down the street, Lisa and Jockey aren't fixing
their wrecked old car that chugs along down the street
with black smoke spilling out of the exhaust
The kids at three and four are always playing outside
the parents do nothing but shout at them
and each other all day long!
They never do as they're told
Jodie goes out drinking, Gareth 'tries' to sing along to his guitar
I have to turn the radio up full blast
I can see all the fallen leaves rustling on the ground
being blown by the wind
flying into the scrapyard of a garden
It's so far away I can hardly see it
The big hills to the right are covered by the light,
fluffy clouds drifting by.

Charlotte Harrison (13)
Crofton High School

Christmas

C hristmas is great
H aving Christmas dinner on your plate
R elatives coming on that date
I t's just great
S anta Claus comes really late
T urkey is the main thing on the plate
M any people laughing but still some dying
A happy time
S uch a merry time when there is no crime.

Mark Walker (12)
Crofton High School

Dreaming

I've swam with the mer-people
Under the sea
Their eyes were like rubies
Staring at me
I've driven a time machine over the stars
Seen Saturn and Jupiter
Pluto and Mars
The red-orange sunshine
Without any peel
Slain dragons and goblins -
But none of it's real
I'm laying in bed as just simply me
I'm not up in space or under the sea
Maybe I'll visit those places again
Where I am the hero
Within my own brain.

Stephanie Hadjioannou (13)
Crofton High School

Aggressive Skating

The wheels are oiled
The wheels are fast
The laces are tied
Snap, the clasps are closed
I'm off again
The wheels are going fast
We go for a 360° then
We go 720° and mute
The adrenaline is flowing
My teeth are snarling
I am the winner.

Lee Rowson (14)
Crofton High School

Eyes Through The Weather

The mood of the god that is the weather, changes again.
Sitting up there upon his throne, he looks down on us all
and decides his plans for the day.
Would it be the eruption of a storm? The light trickle of his nectar
or would he advance his smile upon us all?
Maybe it was because the clouds were bothering him
or maybe it was just because there was no storm that night
to interrupt his lazy sleep.
Whatever the reason for his sudden burst of laughter,
his marvellous smile that morning pierced the muggy clouds
like a knife through butter.
By 12 midday the mood up there changed once again.
Would it be the eruption of a storm? The light trickle of his nectar
or would he advance his smile upon us all?
Maybe it was because the bright gaze of his smile was getting
in his eyes and was obscuring his vision of our world or maybe
it was just because he was in need of a rest.
Whatever the weather's reason for leaving that midday and letting
the brutal attitude of the storm take charge soon he realised
the miserable mood his departure had put our world in.
By 9 at night the weather returned to take charge once again.
Would it be the eruption of a storm? The light trickle of his nectar
or would he advance his smile upon us all?
This time there was no maybe about the situation, he put our world
to rest and simply switched off the light.

Luke Lynam (14)
Crofton High School

Not Really True!

My alarm woke me up at half-past seven,
Another day at school is not exactly Heaven.
But I'll get by I thought to myself,
As I pulled down the cereal off the shelf.
What's wrong with Mum and Dad? They are really upset,
I hope we haven't got another debt.
I'm in the car, I'm on my way,
It's the start of a brand new day.
I'm sitting in the form, no one seems to know,
I'll walk to my class, off I go.
I notice the classroom was empty, but didn't really care,
But I realised why, when out of the window I began to stare.
The funeral of myself was taking place,
I'll never forget the look on my mum and dad's face.
'But I'm here,' I shouted, 'not in that coffin,'
I screamed, I kicked, but no one replied.
I couldn't believe I'd seen my own funeral,
Oh my god! I've gone and died.

Alexandra Robinson (13)
Crofton High School

Slugs And Worms

Slither in the grass
Looking like a piece of ash
Under the leaves they eat away
Gathering in the mud and clay
Sometimes they can't get away

Working hard at their job
Over the seas they get killed by a frog
Wriggling away in and out
Making their home without a doubt
Sometimes they've got to pass away.

Daniel Bird (12)
Crofton High School

Christmas

Christmas time is very near
It only comes once a year
Homeless people cry
As others go happily by.

Christmas Eve is now here
We wait and listen for the reindeer
Snowflakes glisten in the light
On a cold and frosty winter's night.

Christmas Day has now begun
Now the start of lots of fun
The presents we have, are knee-deep
The wrapping paper in a heap.

Boxing Day at last has come
The pantomime will be fun
The whole family will be there
Fun and laughter we will share.

Remember the fun we have had
Also the people who were sad
Remember the fun we had when sharing
It's all about loving and caring.

Thomas Eaton (12)
Crofton High School

The Beach!

It brushes the floor beneath it,
It whispers to and fro,
And charges with its thrashing legs!

They come in many disguises,
And sing if you hold them,
And embed themselves in blankets!

As vicious as a cannibal,
It waits to kill for food,
Like a tiger pouncing on prey!

Sophie Butterworth (12)
Crofton High School

Ten Stitches

The smell of the doctor's sickly sweet,
Like to tell you you're in for a treat.
But how can all this prodding and poking be fun?
I'd rather be out with my friends in the sun.
I hear people crying out with pain,
It's enough to make you go insane.
Walls as grey as a cold winter's day,
Nurses come and go as they may.
I'm sitting on a bed hard as steel,
Needle shoved in as if they don't care how you feel.
Doctors dressed in white from head to toe,
Takes up the needle and begins to sew.
Wait and wait for the pain to set in,
Wait and wait for the torture to begin.
The doctor says he is done,
Ten stitches on each finger and thumb.
No pain was felt,
Just numbness as I knelt,
Upon the doctor's bed of ice.
He uses when slicing and dicing
At his patients when bored.

Rebecca Shaw (13)
Crofton High School

Summer

The flapping crow squawked at the crack of dawn,
Birds sang merrily into the bright sky,
The flowers danced around in the light breeze,
The fiery sun blazed down upon the Earth,
The grass rippled gently in the light breeze,
Fluffy clouds floated dreamily in the sky,
The bright blue sky soon became a dark, dull sky,
The ball of fire evolved to a white sphere.
The wind began to howl outside like a wolf,
A soft hooting noise could be heard in the dark.

Dale Sinnett (12)
Crofton High School

Grim Reaper

Head slasher,
Death maker,
Heaven clasher,
Life taker.

Body halver,
Skull grider,
Limb carver,
Hell finder.

Soul taker,
Evil finder,
Body binder,
Evil maker.

Sam Brear (11)
Crofton High School

My Cat

Peaceful sleeper
Springy pouncer
Mouse catcher
Meat eater

Dog teaser
Smooth jumper
Bird attacker
Children pleaser

Animal spotter
Quick sprinter
Rabbit hunter
Big scoffer.

Emma Thomas (11)
Crofton High School

Tiger

Ball chaser
Fast runner
Forest hunter
Grass hater

Stripe lover
Human stalker
Animal killer
Prey seeker

Friend hater
Sore dater
Love crater
Ugly traitor.

Katie Craig (11)
Crofton High School

Apples

A for apple
Falling from a tree,
So Newton discovered
Just what is gravity.
To take one bite
And fall to the ground,
Snow White realised
Where goodness is found.
Apples of green,
Apples of red,
I think I'll have
A banana instead.

Charlotte Stevenson (14)
Crofton High School

Winter's Here To Stay!

The air so icy and cold,
The sky so dark and grey,
Snow's falling day by day,
Winter's here to stay.

The grass is coated in a blanket of snow,
Many children are out to play,
Snow flying like aeroplanes,
Winter's here to stay.

Dark at morning, dark at night,
Icicles forming day by day,
Waiting patiently for Christmas to come,
Winter's here to stay.

People gathering around an open fire,
Knowing Christmas is on its way,
Everyone's wrapped in scarves and hats,
Winter's here to stay.

There's excitement around, it's Christmas Eve,
And everyone's got plenty to say,
The table it set, the presents are wrapped,
We're all ready for Christmas Day.

Rebecca Mallinder (13)
Crofton High School

Secret

It danced in the strong wind,
like a dainty ballet dancer,
Its leaves tapping the ground,
like someone knocking a door,
It climbed the fluffy clouds,
like hikers climbing a mountain.
Its bright yellow patterns
were as black as night,
And that was the final pansy.

Leanne Hunter (12)
Crofton High School

My Footy Nutter Brother

My brother loves footy,
Although he can be very nutty,
He thinks that Man U rule,
And he's too cool for school.
My footy nutty brother.

My brother's name is Matty,
And he's a black belt in karate.
He can't stand the shops,
So he'll go in a strop,
Because he's my footy nutty brother.

My brother gave the ball a whack,
It zoomed right through midfield and attack.
I watched that ball fly over the wall,
Now he's my footy nutty scorer.

My brother always cheers me up,
Especially when he wins the cup,
Put his footy skills to the test,
To me he'll always be the best.
My footy nutty brother.

Leanne Swift (13)
Crofton High School

Scarecrow

Standing still it watches,
It sways in the wind like a forgotten tale,
But guards the waiting land.
No one cares to think about him,
Or understand his tale.
Day by day he stands
As the world round him spins.
Through the ravaged raven's eye he protects
The land so barren and bare.
No hope for a gentle hand or care
His life lead by fate and despair.

Samantha Brook (12)
Crofton High School

My Bird

Joey is my bird's name,
He's funky, playful and quite tame.
To us he's a little treasure,
And Joey gives us loads of pleasure.

Joey loves to eat his seed,
And he always has it when we feed.
He likes his millet and his chew sticks,
But Joey's the one who has to pick.

He's very lucky he has lots of toys,
And likes to make a lot of noise.
He has some beads that make him chirp,
But sometimes likes to rest on his perch.

He rocks to sleep every day,
All of a sudden he's ready to play.
He breaks his toys, which have to be mended,
But that'll have to wait, Joey's day has ended.

Stephanie Parsons (13)
Crofton High School

The Storm

The wind howled like a dog,
There were delays because of the fog,
The rain pounded on the windows.
The snow fell as fast as bricks.

The moon shone like a bright yellow ball,
The millions of stars stood tall,
The distance was nowhere to be seen
Because of the fog being mean.

The sky was a blanket of clouds
And the ground was a mountain of snow.

Liam Duffy (12)
Crofton High School

Bird Flight

I know it's mad,
But sometimes I would love to be a bird,
Flying through the sky, seeing the world,
Seeing what everyone's up to.
Floating over cities,
Flying over green grass parks,
Soaring swiftly through clouds,
No one to tell you what to do,
What time to come home,
Where you should go, just you, flying by,
Flying up into the sky.
So peaceful, no disruption.
The loud noises of the town left behind.
Darting through a world of blue,
You can see for miles.
Then at night, I fold in my wings,
Cuddle up inside the nest,
Until dawn, when my wings unfold.
The orangey-red sunrise fills the sky,
And I glide and I soar and I float and I dart through the sky . . .

Terri-Anne Jones (11)
Crofton High School

The Bowling Alley

Standing proud, an army of ten,
Waiting for the enemy to attack them again,
Still they stand as enemy nears,
Lack of emotion disguising their fears.

Moving forward, amazing speed,
As fast as a lion with its family to feed,
Keeps moving forward with its enemy in sight,
Then they collide and that is a strike.

They rise again for another round,
The enemy, surely, victory bound.

Gary Woodcock (12)
Crofton High School

Shattered!

A violent break into many small pieces,
The grieving hearts of inconsolable lovers,
The wrecked dream of a wishful youth,
being able to touch but not to feel,
Shedding a tear in the depth of despair,
The failed harvest of a drought stricken country,
The exhausted body of a mountaineer,
The fatigued mind of a troubled student,
The crushed goals of an Olympic hopeful,
For me - midnight approaches,
Drained mind and body still not at rest,
Jumbled thoughts of imperfect homework,
Not satisfied with less than the best.

Ailsa Craig (13)
Crofton High School

The Crocodile

It slithers along the river bank,
Watching prey go by,
Its teeth form a smile,
There's a glint in its eye.

It slowly glides along,
Like a submarine,
Its body submerged in water,
Silent and unseen.

Then a hunter comes along,
The crocodile begins to curse,
The hunter points his gun.
It ends up as a purse!

Kathryn Thorpe (13)
Crofton High School

I'm A Chameleon . . .

I'm a chameleon,
The shine of a star,
The blood in your veins,
I come from afar.

I'm a chameleon,
I capture my prey
With my long, sticky tongue,
What can I say?

I'm a chameleon,
The shade of the floor,
My colour is always changing
From blood-red to the green of an apple core.

I'm a chameleon,
My eyes dart here and there,
I trudge along on my forked feet,
I'm much smaller than a bear.

I'm a chameleon,
So friendly and kind,
I change colour in the sun,
I'm so hard to find!

Beth Chesworth (13)
Crofton High School

The Bird

A giant bird soaring through the sky,
Gradually climbing very high,
Its lights looking like demons' eyes,
A roaring noise as it flies.
Nothing compares to its speedy pace,
The machine's a puma in a race,
But as it rumbles to a halt,
It's like a snail, killed by salt.
Runway all fully clear,
Down comes the plane in its landing gear.

Tom Simpson (12)
Crofton High School

My Brother

I think of my brother as a mate,
He's seventeen going on eight.
He's really funny, always acting the fool,
But if he wants, he can be really cool.
He loves Leeds with all his heart,
He's liked them ever since the start.
If they lose, he gets mad,
Like a dad whose son's been bad.
He likes sitting and watching TV,
His favourite programme is *The Simpsons,* you see.
His eyes are blue like a sparkling sea,
His dark brown hair is always spiky.
His mouth is a box full of pearls,
When he smiles he gets the girls.
He is thin and quite tall,
He is amazing at football.
He is forgiving and very kind,
A better brother you could not find.
I love my brother as much as can be
And I hope he feels the same about me!

Laura Marsh (13)
Crofton High School

My Mobile Phone

This miniature space-age gadget
Looks warm and welcoming
Yet makes a really deafening din.

It holds all my names and numbers
It is my life and soul,
It illuminates the night like street lights.

It keeps me safe and protects me,
With it I can't go wrong,
It is as important to me as my school planner,
If ever I lost it I'd be really quite distraught.

Lauren Russell (12)
Crofton High School

Off To War

Thousands of men
Leave to die,
Death is coming,
We cannot lie.

Grown men crying
Saying goodbye,
Families lost and broken,
We wonder why.

Guns of terror,
Weapons of destruction,
Cries of pain
Like a volcanic eruption.

Tears of the wounded,
Life's filled with sorrow,
People fall asleep for ever,
For them there's no tomorrow.

Why does it have to happen?
Why do people have to die?
No one will say sorry,
Sorry families couldn't say goodbye.

Natalie Gill (13)
Crofton High School

1 Of The 4 Elements Of The World

It sounded like bullets on the window,
Hundreds of glistening eyes on the road,
The windows of the whole house were crying,
Nobody had a smile on their face,
It lay on the sea talking to the beach,
It waited in the clouds, calling us out.
It's a death source, but also a life source,
It's like a present from God and from Hell.
It holds us up and pulls us down, boat, leak.
The element in my poem is water!

Daniel Kane (12)
Crofton High School

Ant Nation

What is one person,
But a ripple in the sea,
But a wave in the desert sands,
But a blade of grass on the giant lawns that we call Earth,
But a heart and conscience of its own?

For in this world right and wrong,
But what is wrong and right without choice or idea?
Indeed without rules,
The ripple in the sea,
The wave in desert sands
And the lone blade of grass
Would perish under one another.

What is one person?
A blink of the world's eye,
The freckle on its mapped-out face,
The carer and destroyer of Mother Nature's lands,
And the future of it all.
One person is but an ant in the way of the world,
But one ant alone cannot succeed.

To answer all of this,
One person is nothing,
But a nation is great.
We should all take a leaf out of the ant's book,
And learn to work as one.

Ruth Greaves (14)
Crofton High School

The Dirt Bike

Roaring loud, ready to go
On any terrain, gravel, snow,
Push the pedal, off it blasts
Moving forward a heavy mass.

Prancing forward at great speed,
It grows hungry and needs to feed,
Killing the environment,
Leaving behind an evil scent.

As fast as a speeding jet,
Held back like a poorly treated pet,
Its face like a pouncing snake,
Its owner is killed as he pulls the brake.

Luke Barratt (12)
Crofton High School

The Car

As I looked down the street,
There it was,
Eyes shining like a cat's
In the night.
It was an angry ghost
Getting me.
It roared as it got close,
Like a mad,
Raging rhinoceros.
Then it screamed,
It was a screaming child.
That was when it
Stopped at the traffic lights.

Matthew Tinsley (12)
Crofton High School

The Knight And The Dragon

Forth he rode from shining city,
Sat astride a beast so proud,
Clad in metal, silver, gleaming,
Cutting through the misty shroud.

Courage, honour, loyalty, strength,
Virtues of the best of men,
For he was a knight of England,
Riding hard for dragon's den.

Climbing down from grey mount's saddle,
Drawing forth his sword from sheath,
Cave mouth gaping in stone cliff face,
Entrance to caverns beneath.

Striding forward into darkness,
Fearless of the fate ahead,
Brave Sir Robin, breathing slowly,
Caught the stench of something dead.

Entering cavern, shouted he,
Raising sword up into air,
'Vile dragon, I have come for thee,
And thou shalt bow to me.'

Dragon rose from darkest shadows,
Lunging forward, lips curled back,
Dragon and brave knight collided,
A battle of bite and hack.

A final swing and dragon fell,
Its massive head sliced clean off,
Robin left the cave the victor,
Mounted great grey stallion,
And rode into the dusk.

Andrew Djokic (12)
Crofton High School

The Rare And Forgotten

Its dainty body so delicate and frail,
Like a lady awaiting someone,
The howling wind chants out its lonely tale,
Its brothers and sisters all gone.

All the giants destroyed its friends,
With their bikes and scaly hands,
Their pollution has destroyed its trends,
Lush green clothes now strands.

Like a person, only less in crew,
More pretty and fragile,
When once was a lot, but now such a few,
The legend tries to smile.

The bang was a meteor landing,
The stem was ruined by someone,
Though it had struggled it had remained standing,
But the last primrose was gone.

Georgina Tate (12)
Crofton High School

Weather!

It beats against the cold window
Like a beating drum
As the cold wind whistles.

It shines up in the bright blue sky
Like a new pound coin
As the big clouds float.

It comes down hard and hits the ground
The shiny ice glistens
As children run inside.

It rumbles in the dark sky
Very loud and scary,
As the white lightning strikes.

Lily I'Anson (12)
Crofton High School

Night Flight

It bolts along with its light flashing,
Roaring like a ferocious lion,
It's a bird soaring high in the night sky.

Inside people are barking like dogs,
They're wolves bickering at their prey.
The aeroplane is dead in its coffin.

Like a gull catching its prey it swoops,
It's faster than the speed of light,
It touches down with full pride in itself.

Like dogs wanting food, people stand up,
They get off the plane very slowly,
The plane is very sad to see them go.

It bolts along with its lights flashing,
Roaring like a ferocious lion,
It's a bird soaring high in the night sky.

Joe Rudge (12)
Crofton High School

The Courtyard

Staring into the empty sky,
Waiting patiently for a new day,
Hoping for the great ball of fire
To shine happiness upon the world before him,
And for it to awaken.
The sleepy world around him,
Hesitating in trepidation,
Like a fly on a spider's web.
And, as the bell of doom cries,
A stampede of vicious animals
Rush over his stone-grey face.
And, as it once again becomes silent,
He stares into the empty sky.

Graham Wardle (12)
Crofton High School

The Park At Night

Trees dance with their crooked arms
And look over me like a tall tower,
By day they're happy, by night evil
And stare at me each and every hour.

The swings scream on their rusty metal
As the wind skips by,
Nobody can predict whether they want us there,
Who, what, when and why?

The slide slopes down dark and wet,
Like a snowy mountain,
Children have fun sliding down
But by night the fun is done.

The grass is long tall snakes
Ready to snap at me,
The park here is an evil place
Let's hope it changes, let's see.

Cathryn Foster (12)
Crofton High School

The Secret Collection

They sit there as good as gold,
Their eyes glistening in the dark like stars,
In their ragged attire.
Some are hiding behind others,
Small, big, miniature, large,
Each one unique
In its own special way.
Some soft, some rough and some smooth,
Some more special than others,
Some have patterns, some don't,
But all are special to me,
My teddy collection.

Victoria George (12)
Crofton High School

Town At Night!

The street lights up
As darkness falls as fast as lightning
But makes no sound in its progress,
The trees are tall
The grass is short,
The litter scatters in the darkness.

As the nights get colder,
The frost starts to bite
Like predators in the misty night,

The shops sit there fast asleep
But the birds fly high into arms so deep.

The roads are wet, dangerous and dark
And end at a big, misty park.

This journey ends as dawn breaks
And the familiar red light falls over the lakes.

Emma Naylor (12)
Crofton High School

Wind

It whistled along the street, like a train
And howled now and then.
It danced between the branches of the trees
Then swiftly crossed the green, waving fields.
It sat by the lake to a soft, smooth breeze
And rested for a while
Then set off like a cheetah once again
And whirled around the shivering bushes.
It sped like lightning to the dark city,
It was the predator on its prey,
It had finally reached its location
But got whipped away by the forceful rain.

Michael Fox (12)
Crofton High School

Cat

Headlights burning brightly,
In the ghostly night,
Illuminating everywhere,
This is his own light.
One long stripe of darkness,
Reaching for the sky,
Swaying gently in the breeze,
The end for his prey is nigh.
Spears pointing sharp and long,
Coming from his face,
Using them to squeeze through gaps,
At a steady pace.
His nose is like a wrinkled button,
Pink and neatly placed,
Sniffs out mice in seconds alone,
Then begins a chase.

Joe Hammond (12)
Crofton High School

My Cat

Her little green eyes sparkle in the light,
When I throw her a cat biscuit, she is not in sight.

I come in at night and turn on the light,
She runs to me in excitement.

We sit together in the armchair whilst I stroke her hair,
Well watching the warm fire glare.

We then both have our tea,
Then she silently purrs on my knee.

She has a snack then lies on her back,
Playing with the biscuit pack.

Sam Railton (13)
Crofton High School

Autumn Leaves Fall

They scuttle and flutter
In a one-legged dance,
Like lightning so fast, they prance,
Tiny elfin dancers,
And those little green leaves
Crisp and brown in autumn, fall
Like rain from the grey sky,
Vast and grey mystery,
So cold and melancholy,
From which falls sparkling rain,
Wet and so refreshing,
On those lovely summer days.
But the rain's unwelcome
On days as cold as these,
So overcast and wintry.
Trees reach out jagged hands,
The snaky grass hisses,
Birds cry like lonely babies.
The outdoor noises scream
And screech, oh so eerily,
While owls wail like howling wind,
But I am safe inside
My warm and loving home,
While the wind whistles so loud.
No harm can befall me
For I'm safe in my home.

Kate Benn (12)
Crofton High School

Summer's Day

On a summer's morning, the light shone,
All the white clouds had left and gone,
The lush green hair began to sway,
Summer had started a brand new day.
The vibrant colours went from side to side,
The trickling water went for a ride.
The bright light shone onto the brown tower,
Casting a black haze on the summer's earth.
A new, vibrant colour was there,
Joining us like a late birth.
A waterfall of feathers came from the brown tower,
They came floating down, then hit the closed-up flower.
The light shone bright until it was night,
Then the garden stood
Such a beautiful sight.

Lauren Fillingham (13)
Crofton High School

It!

Its white skin gets dirty,
Its orange eyes flash on,
Its tail runs along,
Its long nose lights up,
Its feet move smoothly along,
Its black ears stick out,
Its organs are tucked away.
Can you guess what it is?
It is not a mouse,
It is my dad's car.

Hayley Siddall (14)
Crofton High School

The Great Day Out

The sea swaying in ferocious, blistering wind,
To and fro, then back again.
The place where the children play all day long,
Relaxing on the beach, playing ping-pong.

At the funfair throughout the day hanging around
The place I love to play.
Eating an ice cream, thinking about my dream day,
On the beach where I sunbathe.

Running around on the beach all day,
Making my way to the arcade.
As I place the money in the machine,
All that comes out is a penny and a jelly bean.

When the sun goes in,
The lights begin to flash,
All the people come out and spend their cash.

Then in the morning,
It's a brand new day,
And, as usual, children begin to play.

Leanne Crossland (13)
Crofton High School

Parrot!

It says hello when you open the door,
It chats to itself when it's all alone,
It answers the phone with a cheerful reply,
It's never down, it always wants to play,
It dances when the music comes on,
Nodding its head up and down, up and down,
It flies from its cage, backwards and forwards,
It sits on your shoulder and nibbles your ear,
It will give you a peck if you're not wanted near,
It says goodnight when you turn off the light.

Laura Miles (13)
Crofton High School

Best Place In The World

The place where the sun never stops shining,
And tourists never go away,
The place where I love to play and have fun,
Throughout all the day.
The place where I spend lots of time in arcades,
And lose lots of money,
The place where I can relax on the beach with friends,
And have a laugh because it's so funny.
The place where there's lots of nightlife,
And I dance on the disco floor,
The place where I dive in the ocean,
Or walk along the seashore.
The place where I go to funfairs,
With my friends I'll chat,
The place where I eat lots of ice cream,
To make myself fat,
The place where I watch the waves on the tide,
It's the best place in the world.
The seaside.

Shelly Walker (13)
Crofton High School

Poetry

P oetry is a cool thing to write,
O n any subject you can decide,
E very piece has a truthful meaning,
T ry and write some, you'll see what I mean,
R eading poetry is quite exciting,
Y ou are a poet, so have some fun!

Hannah Dawson (13)
Crofton High School

Autumn Days

Days draw to a close,
Clear blue skies die out,
Fluffy pillows no longer float,
Drifting away from the ocean of happiness,
Lit stairways hide away,
In comes the darkness,
The lights have been turned out,
Only torches by the roadside exist,
The dull days last a lifetime,
No shadows can be formed,
Golden carpets cover the floor,
Bright colours have faded away,
Left with only memories of brighter days,
The night is here to stay!

Emma Hunter (13)
Crofton High School

The Bright Light

As I stare out of my window,
I look up there, it is shining down on me.
It is so bright and it seems so low,
The beautiful stars twinkle beside it
With their yellow glisten,
If you be quiet and listen,
You will hear the silence.
The dark blue sky is as blue as the ocean,
The wind sounds like a kettle boiling.
The breeze is shivery,
The wind howls like a wolf,
Don't be fooled by the moon,
You'll see it very soon!

Sarah Magee (13)
Crofton High School

Autumn

They dance in the wind,
As it whistles and hums,
The sky bangs
Like loud, beating drums,
Their confused children
Scurry fast down the hill,
Rolling promptly
Their crinkled eyes fill.

As autumn comes near,
Their branches appear bare,
Kids float off,
As they thin and tear,
Branches grow more slowly,
And they start to snap,
Now alone,
It begins to nap.

Samantha Bryan (12)
Crofton High School

Lonely

It sat there all alone,
Whistling as time went by,
Its great, big, long, thin roots
Reflected by its branches.
Reaching out for freedom,
Everlasting sunshine.
Midnight fell in the sky,
The wind howled fiercely,
The mist fell upon the tree,
Another day had passed.

Charlotte Bettison (13)
Crofton High School

The Beach

As I sit on the sandy beach,
I listen to the noise,
Swish, swash, and it sounds
Like the whirling wind.
I look ahead,
I can see children playing
And hear them screaming.
Far away we see boats
Struggling after the waves,
Then, all of a sudden, a storm occurs,
The boats overturn and go out of sight.
Then the fog comes along,
Like a flash from a camera,
The tide comes in,
Nobody lies on the beach,
No children can we hear,
Still we listen to the noise,
Swish, swash.

Nicola Foster (13)
Crofton High School

My Favourite Thing

Its eyes like coal,
Its big black cave,
And the button just above it.
The long, pink snake that comes out of the cave,
When it wakes me on a morning,
Its skin all hairy and fluffy,
Its small, stumpy tail,
Its round belly,
Its feet like stones,
Its big floppy ears,
Its playful personality,
Its joyful spring and jump,
Its facial expressions when it's in a mood.

Lauren Turner (13)
Crofton High School

Trains

The concrete is as cold as ice,
The seats are made out of hard metal,
People are talking excitedly.
It whistles like the wind when it comes,
People jump, people push,
People stare and people look,
Sometimes hurrying as though there's no tomorrow,
Lots of noise and lots of chatter.
Some complain,
Some go quietly,
Some people have bags,
Some people have nothing,
But they all have a tale to tell.

Elizabeth Evans (14)
Crofton High School

The Sea

Its golden granules of salt
Sparkle in the burning sun,
The clashing sounds like loud cymbals
Belting against the rough rocks,
Children with their spades and buckets,
Seagulls screeching in the sky,
A cruise ship in the far distance,
Swimming closer and closer.
The sea as blue as sapphire,
And sand as soft as cotton!

Hayley Gaunt (13)
Crofton High School

The Creature's Flight

It powers to a roaring start,
Goes to the running track,
Then races as fast as lightning,
And leaps into the air.

Once in the air, it soars higher,
It spreads its wings for height,
Sometimes it shakes in mid flight,
It glides like an eagle.

With its gigantic steel wings,
It stops thunderously,
It glides to a landing,
And speeds to a building.

Machines cut into its side,
People inside set free,
The creature left exhausted,
Machines come and feed it.

The aeroplane was this creature.

Joshua Cleland (13)
Crofton High School

Raging Beast

Like a bull, you are wild,
Or can be made tame,
But often you escape,
Send people insane.

Nobody likes you now,
You're changing people,
You convert from gentle
To cruel and vicious.

You're a terrible thing,
You might like to know
Your name, it is Anger,
Just leave, depart, go.

Matthew Bradley (13)
Crofton High School

Crocodile Features

A long, slow line of leather,
Green and brown, all but dead.

A razor smile of icy teeth,
A broad corrugated back.

As tough as bark, like a tree trunk,
Half submerged by water.

Above the jaws set like traps,
Fathers dangle their babies' legs.

Dragon breath is smouldering,
Bubbling up from the snout.

One careless kick,
Or heartbreaking slip.

And that huge mouth
Will split apart like a flick knife.

Ross Leith (13)
Crofton High School

Winter Poem

Leaves flutter through harsh air,
And people's hair, as cold as ice.
Feels like a mummy
When wrapped up warm,
Toes all tingly,
Fingers numb.
Floor cracks when you touch it,
As fragile as glass.
Trees shed their long coats,
In the cold.
Flowers die,
In the snow.

Peter Goult (14)
Crofton High School

Goal!

James gets the ball,
He has no clue at all,
Hoofs the ball up field,
Policeman uses his shield.

The throw is taken,
The Turkey defence is shaken,
Owen runs and crosses,
Sven's counting his losses.

Now it's a free kick,
James is doing a trick,
Gerrard is taking,
Turkey's wall is shaking.

Gerrard has hit it,
Sven's getting fit,
It hits the net,
Becks lost his bet,
And it's a fantastic *goal!*

Chris Lewis (13)
Crofton High School

The Flying Machine

It glides through the sky like a bird in flight,
It glistens in the sun,
It sits dormant on the black tarmac,
It runs beneath the clouds,
It glides round the world over sea and sky,
With the sun, sea and sand.
Fast or slow doesn't matter, still a comfy ride.
America or Spain,
Gliding round and round over sunset sky,
The plane we all fly in.

Hannah Richardson (13)
Crofton High School

The Classroom

Dark as my attic,
It is as gloomy as the midnight fog,
It smells like a wet dog,
It is as dull as a spot of ink,
It is a graveyard,
It is as old as the Earth,
It feels like you are trapped in a box,
It is scary when it is locked,
It is like the doors are blocked,
It is sweaty and cramped,
It is boring when the teacher blabs on.
The classroom!

Craig Mosley (11)
Crofton High School

Supermarket

As I entered
The arms of people grabbed me,
They wouldn't let me go,
So I struggled for the key.

I dropped to my feet,
It hurt me as if I'd fallen on a tree,
I could feel something hard and smooth,
I picked it up,
It was as heavy as iron.

It felt like varnished wood,
But was it the key?

Louise Grogan (11)
Crofton High School

Hunter

A dark shape in the night,
A rustle in the grass,
Golden eyes shining,
Full of grace and class.

Tiny ears twitch,
What was that?
It's nothing, calm down,
The mouse thinks from where it sits.

The figure moves again,
Crouching close to the ground,
A hunter in the dark
Never to be found.

There it is again,
That crackle of the leaves,
The mouse begins to run now,
Through blades of grass it weaves.

The hunter's pace now quickens,
Then muscles coil like springs,
It leaps, soars through the air,
Flying without wings.

Sharp claws tear through flesh,
Insides spill like toys' stuffing,
A squeal of pain in the blackness
And then . . .
Nothing.

Emma Marshall (13)
Crofton High School

Who Are You?

A soft rustle,
Like wind through a tree,
A bright eye,
A jewel in the dark,
A chirp of recognition,
    Who are you?

A *click, click, click,*
Like the tapping of feet,
A soft rush of air,
Wind breathing on a cheek,
Looking in your direction,
    Who are you?

Swoop to the ground,
Graceful in flight,
Gleaming bright feathers,
Heads turned towards you,
A hoot of delight,
    Who are you?

An owl full of joy,
An owl full of grace,
An owl in flight,
An owl on the hunt,
An owl to its prey.

Danielle Jowett (13)
Crofton High School

Going Home

Briskly walk through cold, dark streets,
The wind begins to roar,
Then finally I reach my goal,
I see my own front door.

My house is cold and unwelcoming,
It's been lonely and empty all day,
Still I discard my coat and bag,
And with them the stress of my day.

I hastily put my fire on,
House now feeling more like a home.
The candles and television are next,
Not forgetting to plug in the phone.

Swamped in my fluffy dressing gown,
I relax in my flumpy armchair,
Feet still like blocks of ice from the endless walk home,
So I toast them by the fire with care.

I'm fully relaxed like a contented cat,
I sip my hot chocolate with glee,
I'm watching my favourite film again,
As I wait for my microwaved tea.

Catherine Millar (13)
Crofton High School

Death

More silent than a sleeping widow,
As stealthy as a stalker's shadow
And when she creeps round through the night,
You're gonna see a sorry sight.
As pale as a sheet of paper,
She could get you now or get you later
I hope you've taken in all I've said,
Cos when she visits, you'll be dead!

Bradley Shepherd (12)
Crofton High School

What Is The Moon . . . ?

I think that the moon is a silvery puddle
Or a jet-black bank of earth,
It gradually dries up to nothing,
But then the process is reversed.

Or could it be a solitary sequin,
Sewed upon the blackest cloth,
Prepared for a princess of darkness
Or the wings of a beautiful moth?

Or could it be a precious coin,
Left lying in a leather purse,
Minted of the finest silver,
For when the weather is at its worst?

Or could it be a single snowflake
Trapped before it could fall?
And now it's floating in the night sky,
A friendly face for us all.

They say it's made of green cheese,
But his I think is cheap,
I think God's left the landing light on,
Just to help me fall asleep.

Rachel Crookes (13)
Crofton High School

Supermarket

I walked in on my own
I could see robots
My trolley was as slow as a slug
Weaving in and out
Tins were standing like army men
I could hear the tills clicking
I was as scared as Shaggy
I could see the sun smiling down on me
It was like Jurassic Park III
I was so green I was like the Incredible Hulk.

Kyle Turner (11)
Crofton High School

The Weather Dragon

It was an awful day in Wakefield,
There was not a ray of sun to behold,
Only darkness, shadow and grey,
It was a very depressing day.
The weather dragon has appeared,
Terror is filling the midday sky,
His ferocious face peers through the clouds.
The thunder crashes with every beat of his wings,
His chilling breath bends trees almost double.
His claws of lightning strike the ground,
His gaping jaws bite people's skin,
With icy teeth of hailstones.
The people run into their homes,
And hide from the evil dragon's wrath.
They put on hats and scarves and gloves,
And hide under umbrellas and shelters.
Waiting and waiting till the dragon disappears,
His anger abated, his fury at rest,
'Til he recuperates his energy,
And peacefully rests and plans his next attack.

Barney Horner (12)
Crofton High School

Monkey

Tree climber
Quick mover
Banana snatcher
Great thinker
Little tinker
Hairy creature
Playful friend
Round the bend.

Rebecca Gent (11)
Crofton High School

What Has The World Come To?

The fields used to be full of lush grass and
Insects big and small,
But now they are full of old bottles and litter and
There is no fresh grass at all.

The trees used to be home to owls and
Bearing lots of fruit,
But now they're cut down to build factories and homes and
You'll never hear the owls hoot.

There used to be peace in the world where
Adults didn't fight but play,
But now when I turn on the TV,
There's a war going on every day.

I wish that we could go back
To the way the world used to be,
Where everyone lived with each other
In perfect harmony.

What has the world come to?

Sam Brady (13)
Crofton High School

F1 Saturday

Faster than a cheetah,
Racing down the track,
They keep on going,
Never looking back.

The cars keep speeding,
Speeding away,
All 72 laps,
Every other Saturday.

Michael Schumacher,
Eddie Irvine,
Breaking down, going in to the pit,
Back on track - just in time!

Samantha Cleland (14)
Crofton High School

The Rampage

You could see it from a mile away.
Coming closer and closer,
You could feel the temperature turn for the worse,
The streets were silent and empty, we knew this was coming,
Crofton was dead.
You could hear the rubbish blowing and the leaves rustling
Getting louder and louder as it came closer and closer.
The noise picked up,
And suddenly,
The wind rampaged through Crofton as if a giant had stood on it,
Its destructive path was clear,
The fierce and menacing gale slaughtered everything in its way,
Not just people,
However,
Suddenly the rubbish stopped blowing
And the leaves stopped rustling,
And the gale passed before you knew it,
Like a speeding train.

Daniel Le Page (12)
Crofton High School

Graveyard

Love breaker,
Spirit saver,
Body bearer,
Widow maker.

Breath taker,
Heart pounder,
Shadow dweller,
Nightmare maker,

Spooky screamer,
Life holder,
Night whisperer,
Sadness leaver.

Jennifer Ward (11)
Crofton High School

The Thing

You could see it creeping up on us,
Getting darker and darker,
Then - it began,
The temperature suddenly turned,
Streets were silent and empty,
It was here,
The storm had begun.
Rain came like never before,
Wind howled like a pack of hungry wolves,
Hailstones hit you like chunks of rock,
Dustbins were knocked over,
Cars tipped in the flinch of a moment,
Pouncing from rooftop to rooftop,
The thing grew bigger and bigger every second,
Pulling off chimneys and tiles,
People screaming,
Running for their doors,
Animals scurrying for their holes and nests,
Protecting their young,
People who were left
Stood in amazement
As they watched it destroy
Their town.
Then, all of a sudden,
As if it had died,
It stopped,
Leaving the village wrecked in minutes,
Homes ruined,
The town flooded.

Josh Wood (12)
Crofton High School

Here We Go Again

Here comes the lecture
Like a record playing,
Over and over again.
'Don't do that! Grow up! Have more respect!'
I've heard it all before
It's becoming a bore.
Why all the pressure?
What's the rush to become an adult?
To have some maturity in your life?
Like a lead weight on your shoulders,
Such a burden!
I'm gonna grow up eventually it's certain
But until that day . . .
In every way . . .
I'm gonna act irresponsible
So my parents find this *talk* impossible!

Cheryl Chapman (12)
Crofton High School

What Is Yellow?

Yellow is the gleaming sun
And the summer sunflowers.
Yellow is a bunch of fresh bananas,
Hanging on a market stall.
Yellow is a tennis ball,
Bouncing around on a tennis court.
Yellow is a block of cheese
And the get ready traffic light.
Yellow is a burning fire,
Shining out of a blazing chip pan.
Yellow is a Cif bleach bottle,
Which cleans my yellow downstairs toilet.

Hannah Blagg (12)
Crofton High School

The Waging Water Dwarfs

The whole of Wakefield came to a stand,
The day the mighty dwarfs came.
An army of those little devils,
Marched up an down the road.

They reached the centre and pulled out their hoses,
And that was the end of the town centre.
They marched quickly on the town theatre,
They smashed the stage and left the crowd crying.

'Those menacing pipes must be stopped!'
Shouted a brave survivor from the crowd.
So this brave survivor armed his men,
With many umbrellas and wooden rafts.

So this mighty army sailed through disaster
And were on the search for these tiny terrorists.
Once they reached the end of the line,
It surely must be over.

The survivors gave battle to these mean machines,
They were bombarded with water bombs.
They believed the whole thing would come to an end,
When suddenly all the water drained.

All these mighty water dwarfs,
Came to the end of their lives.

Michael Channer (12)
Crofton High School

The Creature Of The Night

When I go upstairs to bed,
I dare not go to sleep,
The creature of the night creeps down
And hides things in my mind.
It makes me look like I'm diseased
And my emotions come alive,
To grow inch by inch each night of the week,
I just can't seem to stop,
I lose more friends and gain more foes,
Than you could ever imagine,
My life is over or so it seems,
Will this ever stop?
My bigger brother says it will,
I don't think I believe him,
This has now gone on for months,
The creature makes my voice go squeaky,
The horror had better stop soon,
I cannot take this, help me please,
I need to get away,
The world is crumbling all around me,
Piece by piece I lose it,
The creature's getting ever crueller,
I feel like I will die,
I go to bed four foot ten
And wake up five foot high.

John Dobson (12)
Crofton High School

The Weather Wages War On Wakefield

The ice-cold figure appeared,
Out of the mist,
It was a horrifying and deceiving shape.
Like a boulder it came big and strong,
Full of destruction.
Closer towards town it crept,
Parading with vicious looking eyes.
It was obese and treacherous,
Just like a villain demolishing everything in its path
In front of this beast was a shield of lightning,
Blasting for all to see.
The roaring and bawling could be heard for miles around.
Closer it got to Sandal Castle,
Bringing with it bleak and drab weather.
It disrupted the townsfolk with a sense of forceful fear.
An ugly and menacing face appeared,
With water running down it.
I got out my raincoat and umbrella,
They were my armour and shield.
I kept on marching to the beast, full of hope,
I chased it out of town, away it went,
I won the war against the rain.

Laura Turner (12)
Crofton High School

Street Lights

Have you ever wondered
Who turns the street lights on,
It could be God, it could be Miss
It could be even Mum.

It can't be God who turns them on
As he is far too busy,
He has to make the world spin round,
He must be very dizzy.

Keri Cawthra (13)
Crofton High School

The Singing Lark

Dawn breaks for the singing lark,
Her beak so soft, her feathers dark.
The only sound that was to be heard,
Is the voice of this magnificent bird.
Her solemn brown eyes stare from above,
For this is the creature of desperate love.
Her beautiful wings glide so low,
But her heart is full of joy and sorrow.
She spontaneously leaps from branch to nest,
She's flown back and forth, east to west.
She swifts her head from side to side,
Her feathered tail gently glides.
She opens her beak, so slender, so long
And then pronounces her special song.
The song is soft, the song is dark,
It is the song of the singing lark.

Danielle Louise Hall (12)
Crofton High School

My Car

Its bright eyes light up,
As I enter,
Softly purring away,
Waiting patiently like a dog,
For me to start it up
And eventually we reach, in sunset,
The windy, stony road.

Its eyes still blinding,
Bright and afraid,
Then I go slow,
Push down with my foot, on the pedal
As we carry on, on the road again.

Sarah Cowan (11)
Crofton High School

The Weather Wages War On Crofton

The army was throwing spears of heat
And everyone was defending themselves by using sun lotion.
The corporal realised we were tough,
So he sent them marching in.
Suddenly there was rumbling,
Like a volcano ready to explode.
The rain was people's tears,
Victims of war.
More thundering orders came forth,
Machine guns killing off the sun.
He sent the poisonous gases leaking,
We retreated back home.
As we lay in bed,
Our bunkers for the night,
The sky was flashing,
The wind was howling like a wolf.
The next day came,
Sooner than wanted.
We had no choice but to fight back,
With our warm woolly scarves and hats.
He battered and he bashed,
But he didn't get through.
As suddenly as his attacks arose,
He became weaker and weaker and weaker.
All was safe for now,
The guard has dropped.
But still an eerie presence lay,
Amongst all the carnage he created.
Maybe it was the white flag,
Or deception of the mind.

Lucy Brown (12)
Crofton High School

Death

He's been to every war and battle
He's seen every face and thing
He's that sweet relief
That pain and terrible time
He's hated by every woman and man
The children's nightmare around
He's just a misunderstood worker
Who's just trying to do his job
He's there when you don't know it
Probably near you now
He strikes when the time is right
No telling when he comes for you
He's a friend of the elderly
And of those with mean disease
He's a silent shifty shadow
With his way he'll win
If he doesn't get you now
He's getting you later
But don't be scared, *Death* isn't arriving soon!

Sam Cook (12)
Crofton High School

Cat Kenning

Rat catcher
Food muncher
Mouse chaser
Bird snatcher
Great pouncer
Long sleeper
Deep breather
Fish teaser.

Daniel Jones (11)
Crofton High School

The Fair Game

As they stood staring at us giving us the eye of death,
They tried to intimidate us like a ferocious lion
And a helpless young mouse.

The referee blew the whistle
We knew we were the underdogs to a team like this.
Their passing as sharp as broken glass
And their strength as hard as an upset rhino.

Although we were the underdogs we were 100% committed
To winning this game and determined to come out on top.

We watched their top players like a bird watcher
Who had just seen a very rare bird.
The game was very even but they were the ones on top.
0-0
We were tiring every minute.
We had a last kick of the game.
It was all going to change.

A brilliantly taken corner with a well placed header.
A top corner goal and a goal of the month contender.
Our supporters went wild as the final whistle blew.
The opposition were broken-hearted
But congratulated us on our performance.

Luke Duffy (13)
Crofton High School

Wolf

Swift eyes that can see in the dark,
The terrifying voices that howl and bark
Ears that can hear the lightest breeze,
It makes me shiver to my knees.
Teeth that are as sharp as a knife
And legs that run to save my life.
I look back but all I see,
Is their glowing eyes staring back at me.

Victoria Connelly (11)
Crofton High School

Sneaky Snake

The sneaky snake is sly and shy,
He creeps round the school hoping not to die.
He's like an animal never discovered
And lurches in the shadows,
So's not to be spotted.

He only comes out when the coast is clear,
But quickly leaves and disappears.
He's like a person in a vanishing act
And he's the one that vanishes just like that.

He uses cracks in the walls
To slink past pupils from floor to floor
And when it's time to go home,
He lingers in the corner his face all a gloom.
He never comes out to play,
Not even in the middle of May,
It's like he's never seen the light of day.

He is the sneaky snake.

Gareth Ventom (13)
Crofton High School

Dolphin

Playful swimmer
soft squeaker
fish eater
excellent swimmer
blue sea diver
bottle-nosed and friendly
feelings senser
cute and cuddly
tail flapper.

Lauren Jones (11)
Crofton High School

Treacherous Tiger Torches Town

Prowling in and out of streets
Rapid rain storms forming
Then the noise begins to grow
Roaring winds are rigid
High Ackworth here he goes
Throwing thunderous thunderstorms
Pouncing on the rooftops
As the pouring begins to come
Clambering up the hillside
Quick lash of hailstones
As he makes the clouds turn black
With an almighty launch
Starting to approach my house
He turns with a powerful glare
Flashing by every house
A sudden silence grows
With a peep of golden light
As the fairies begin to spread a golden sheet of sunlight.

Heather Cavill (12)
Crofton High School

Dogs

Energetic and playful
Happy and fun
Fast or slow
Old or young

Big or small
Timid or shy
Sharp teeth and claws
What am I?

Ashleigh Jowett (11)
Crofton High School

Through My Window

Through my window straight ahead I can see
A field where people saunter with their dogs and cycle across
On the left running straight through there is a train flying past
Something is different
I don't know what
Maybe it's just because it's hot
And I can see a confusing ripple in the sky and
Wait
I can smell it
It's a barbecue for tea tonight
Sometimes if I'm quiet
I can see
Small birds picking at the food people have left out for them
I can also see John next door chopping at his unbelievably bulky lawn
Once again the sun blazes down on my face
And blinds me for an instance
But then I can see again.

Simon Cudlip (14)
Crofton High School

View Out Of The Window

As I gaze out the window the sun peers over the rooftops,
Waking the residents from their peaceful slumber.
The wind swirls round the trees,
Pulling lifeless shapes up into the clouds.
As always, young Nicola scurries across the pavement,
Eager to fulfil her errands,
Her mother peering out of the window waiting for her return.
One by one each curtain twitches, revealing its inhabitants,
Waiting for their day to begin.
Vehicles start to clutter up the streets,
Delivering the children who are ready and eager to learn.
The same thing happens every morning,
But what happens next no one can tell.

Jade Bannister (13)
Crofton High School

She Was Gone

She chose to walk alone,
Though people wondered why,
Refused to look forwards,
Eyes cast upwards, towards the sky.
She didn't have companions,
No need for earthly things,
Only wanted freedom,
From what she felt were puppet strings.
She longed to be a bird,
So she might fly away,
She pitied every blade of grass,
For planted it would stay.
Some say she wished too hard,
Some say she wished too long,
But we woke one autumn day, to find that . . . she was gone.
The trees they say stood witness,
The sky refused to tell,
But someone who had seen it,
Said the story played out well.
She spread her arms out wide,
Breathed in the break of day,
She just let go of what she held
And then . . . she flew away.

Sophie Roscoe (14)
Crofton High School

The Wind

Hat pincher,
Skirt lifter,
Tree destroyer,
Hair ruiner.

Victoria Phillips (11)
Crofton High School

View From A Window

Straight ahead I can see the sun rising,
Bringing the world alight.
To the left of the sun, there sits beautiful blackbirds,
Welcoming this great ball of fire.
Today snow lay freshly upon the fence,
Glistening and shining like diamonds.
Sometimes every now and then the sun's melting the snow,
Breaking the white blanket that encased the world in sleep.
The binmen break the silence of the air,
They plough the bins through the ice.
People pass by cautiously with their dogs,
Wishing they were home and dry.
Flowers awaken from their dewy sleep,
A cat prowls along the brick wall,
Racing home for breakfast.
The horse across the road in the field,
Trots off for some hay,
Wanting to line its stomach with food.
The air looks cold and crisp.
Mr and Mrs Jones come out to de-ice their car,
Mr Holsworth peering from behind the curtains,
Shaking his head at the pigeon feathers on the lawn.

Amy Worth (13)
Crofton High School

The Cat

Mouse catcher
Bird snatcher
Rat chaser
Claw scratcher
Meat muncher
Long sleeper
Milk lapper
Height lover.

Nicholas Hadjioannou (11)
Crofton High School

View From A Window

Ahead of me
I see the houses of my elders,
My sister
Playing football on the old railway,
The woman next door has collected her washing
For the first time
Sometimes I hear infants
Grappling in the street

Shape-shifting clouds are filled with darkness
A storm is brewing,
The rain bouncing off the ground
Like repeating bobs of a ping-pong ball

The cold is winging its way north,
My sister hurries in, drenched
As though she'd taken a trip through a car wash.
Night settles in

In the distance I see flashing lights
From a plane no bigger than a full stop
And the twinkling brightness of the stars
Like the sun's reflection in a mirror

The dogs in the yard barking and howling
Like ravenous wolves
The wind picks up and the sky clears
It's a new day.

Lauren Cooper (13)
Crofton High School

A View From A Window

Ahead of me I see,
The bending, twisting street with people scurrying by.
To the left there are,
Rows of houses like books on a bookshelf.
Kids shriek in the street, lamp posts towering high.
The man from down the road is not stood talking
To the people passing by,
I wonder where he could be?
Sometimes I see Steve and Martin
Kicking the football to each other in the street,
Showing off to the people driving by.
I can see,
The tall, bare trees, their branches like fingers,
Leaves are fluttering around.
The wind is getting up,
Night is drawing in.
I see cats sneaking by,
Prowling for their prey,
Dogs barking as if talking to each other.
On the horizon I see clouds, like mountains,
Big and black.
A plane thunders by,
Lights flashing, flying like a bird.

Gabrielle Thomas (13)
Crofton High School

Ballerina

Gracefully twirls
Diamonds and pearls
Elegant dancer
Reindeer prancer
Tutu wearer
Flower carrier
Music maker
Audience lover.

Natalie Fox (11)
Crofton High School

True Secrets

Through my cold caravan window,
I stare into the whirling, blue North Sea.
But it isn't blue.
Green, brown, blue, black
Stirred together to create
This ice-cold lashing whip.
But the real secret,
Of the sea,
Is the torment
It creates.
In winter it swells
Bigger than ever seen before.
It tickles and torments cliff sides
Ripping . . .
Slashing . . .
Tearing
Like a tornado tearing up the next innocent village.
It scoops great rocks, the size of garden sheds,
Tossing them about like a beach ball
To each of the following waves.
After winter it dies
To a subtle washing beach cleaner.

Lois Gore (13)
Crofton High School

Ball

Window smasher,
Belly basher.

Entertainer,
Car crasher.

High bouncer,
Speedy roller.

Loud squeaker,
Light floater.

Paige Ashcroft (11)
Crofton High School

View From A Window

As the sun rises in the morning
I gaze upon the garden
There's the sun that's peeking over the hill
Highlighting the dew drops
Like individual crystals on a green silk dress.
The trees at the bottom of the garden
Casting shadows of darkness
The neighbours cursing the day they'll have
After the perfect weekend they've had
Rushing to their car to escape
From the quiet road
To the bustle of the busy town.
In the distance the smoke from the power station
Spirals like a tornado
Mrs Grice steps out and looks at the sky
Breathing in the clean, fresh air.
Her hair floating like angels in the breeze
Mr Linton jump-starting his banger of a car
Little children scurrying down the road
Like a swarm of bees searching for someone to sting,
With wondering mothers gabbing about all the gossip.

Claire Thompson (13)
Crofton High School

Kenning

Nifty swimmer,
Sometimes floater,
Sly stinger,
Arms all over,
Pink oozer,
Daunting drifter,
Saboteur muncher,
Transparent twister!

A mysterious underwater jellyfish.

Hannah Yates (11)
Crofton High School

My Life Poem

Time to start another day,
All my tears just fade away,
Last night power,
Today unsure,
It's all over, there is no more,
The anger, confusion, endless dismay,
I pray and hope for a better day,
Terrorists attack, it's on the news,
More and more killings and abuse,
A car passes,
A mouse scurries by,
Nothing matters, I don't quite know why,
The journey to school, is boredom hello!
My mate Danni, oh I don't know,
I get to school ready to face the day,
Go through the gates there's no way out,
They keep us caged like a dangerous species,
The bossy, the moody
The boy who cries wolf,
The show off, the nasty
The queen of all hearts,
All put together makes the room of all terror
There's no turning back I'm at the end of my tether!

Stephanie Smith (13)
Crofton High School

Snake

Sleek, stealthy killer
Graceful, deadly hunter
Frightened cowards, scared hider
Curling coiler
Living egg layer
Powerful, suffocating constrictor
Lethal biter
Ultimate heat-seeker.

Matthew Lingard (11)
Crofton High School

View From A Window

Straight ahead I see the old lady opposite staring out of her window
peeking through the gap in the curtains.
She can stand there for hours just staring at the neighbours,
expressionless.
Never talks, never smiles, just stares.

To the left the cheerful Davina mowing her bright green lawn
very enthusiastically
To the right I can see Simon washing his already very clean car
barking at his son like a dog.

Autumn leaves from Jerry's tree are blowing along the street
like they have a mind of their own, twisting and turning.

Sometimes you can see my brother and his joyful friends
doing kiddie things in the street, crashing into each other
every so often and tears fall from their eyes like waterfalls.

Something is different today, it is very quiet,
usually the street is filled with deafening, noisy children
squealing and screeching at one another.

Yesterday's newspaper rolls across my garden,
two girls' faces staring at me from the front cover.
No more kiddie games for them.

Laura Marsh (13)
Crofton High School

My Rabbit

Fast scuttler
Great chewer
Food nibbler
Thirsty drinker
Love sharer
Fantastic starer
House builder.

Rebecca Morton (11)
Crofton High School

Canal Boat

I look outside the side hatch
And see fish swimming free,
Young and old people walking,
Look a little at me.

As we cut through the water,
A pool of boys jumping in,
The engine's going,
A man is mowing,
To the left of me.

Conkers falling to the ground,
Dogs shake off all the muck,
My naughty puppy running riot,
People stop and stare!

Then I start to argue with my sister,
Over something so stupid,
I lash out towards her,
She screams for Mum to come,
I get told off and so does she.

Morgan Raby (13)
Crofton High School

The Lion

Free, wild runner,
Shaggy, rough growler,
Hungry, desperate meat eater,
Quiet, sly camouflager,
Fast, tough hunter,
Strong, powerful leaper,
Mean, fierce pouncer,
Sharp clawed trapper,
Determined skin ripper,
Helpless antelope killer,
Glad, successful winner,
Clever running master.

Luciana Nelson (11)
Crofton High School

A View From A Window

I can see lots of houses where I notice
The man over the fence sneakily smoking outside
So he doesn't contaminate the air around his children.
To the left there are people's gardens
But not much happens in them.
Except for the one next door
Where the little boy called Matthew comes out to play.
Every day after school he's such a funny sight
He's always bounding up and down on his own
Talking to himself while his dad bellows at him
For doing something wrong every five minutes.
But today he has not appeared
Neither can I hear his dad's bellowing.
Sometimes he is a little storm trooper
Or a secret agent, depending on what he's playing
I can hear him yelling and making gun noises.
He also plays fighting games and goes to Cubs
But most of the time he's on his own.
I wonder why his mum never seems to be around
It's as if she doesn't care
I feel as if I should do more to help him.
What happens at home when he's not alone,
Why does he look so scared when his dad's around?
It seems as if he's done something wrong again.

Amy Simpson (14)
Crofton High School

Why You?

As I see you stood with friends
I see the real you,
When you walk by a funny feeling runs down my spine,
Even though you hurt me deep down inside.
Everyone knows me now because of you,
But as days pass, things seem fine for now.
I don't want to show weakness,
So I'm gonna smile and tell the whole world I'm fine.
I'll keep my distance from now on,
But deep down inside where no one can hear me,
I'll be calling for you.
Why do I love you like I do?
Like I always will.
I don't even want to.

Laura Atkinson (13)
Crofton High School

Lazy Afternoon From My Window

The trees blow in the breeze,
The golden, crisp leaves gently sway to the ground,
The pond shimmers while the ducks swim on by.

Children hunt for conkers under the golden sheet of leaves,
Dogs hurry by, collecting sticks for their owners,
Sarah and Steve collect the leaves from the dying grass.

Horses gallop around, nibbling the grass,
Planes fly by, like a snail leaving a white trail of smoke,
Jane and Mark were arguing as they arrived home early from work.

My mum struggles to peg the washing out,
Children run inside as the church bells ring for dinner time,
The car struggles to start as my dad pushes it out of the garage.

Rebecca Hogan (14)
Crofton High School

The War Of The Weather

A rumble of thunder came from afar,
The sound is creeping closer
A flash of lightning fills the black night sky.
The sound is reaching Sharlston
A loud howl of sharp icy breeze
The enemy is here.

Approaching the centre of the village
Feeling the air rumble and shake
The daggers of rain splash to the ground
Feeling the rain, wet and sharp
As the rain pounces down and turns into hail
Feeling the stones, cold and piercing.

I'm stood alone, my only shield is my umbrella
A crash of lightning knocks down a lamp post
The wind roars louder and louder
Like a warrior he fires a thud of thunder
As he thumps up and down the streets
Laughing and giggling, making Sharlston shake.

It carries on throughout the night
As children run to the windows
The warrior terrorises the small village
Morning breaks through the grey, dismal clouds
The sun's blazing rays frighten the warrior away
He beckons and cowers away into the mist.

Charlotte Nunn (12)
Crofton High School

View From A Window

As the morning approaches people open windows into their lives,
reluctantly pull back the curtains and the show begins.
To the left are the Marshes, Steve makes an earlier start,
kisses his wife goodbye and drives off into the distance,
his small red car becoming just a mere smudge on the clear horizon.
Straight in front of me are the Lavignes,
April, the gossip, has assumed her watching position
and by now is clinging comfortably to the pink curtains
In her front room, her pink dressing gown camouflaging her
away from the people, as she watches everyone with her eagle eye.
Slowly but surely sounds seep through the walls as Kelsie,
the baby in the house to the left, is woken from her peaceful slumber,
her shrill scream pierces the air as she shows her appreciation
for her mother snatching her away from the warm comfort of her cot.
One after another engines are fired up as the provider of the house
sets out to work.
In every house snuggled into the cul-de-sac is a family desperate
to hide away from those who feed on the deep, dark secrets
everyone has, that somehow manage to be found out.

Hannah Lockwood (13)
Crofton High School

The Car

Bright eyes blinking in the darkness,
Purring loudly in the cold.
Reaching the road like a stumbling creature,
Street lights of solid gold.

Leading the way down stony streets,
Chugging slowly as it moves.
Trotting like a black horse in the bitter cold,
Wheels like rubber hooves.

The glaring windows fully close,
And guard the car through the night.
And now the creature sleeps and rests peacefully,
No longer eyes so bright.

Helen Brown (12)
Crofton High School

Birthday Dreaming

I woke up to hear the birds sing
Waiting for this wonderful day to begin
I jumped out of bed, hit the floor with a thump
I grabbed for the door but fell with a bump.

I ran down the stairs and into the room
Knowing I'd open my presents soon.
My sister came in with bags of cuddles
She was being nice, my brain was in muddles.

My mum came in with bacon and eggs
But my brother kicked me in the legs.
He shouted, 'Here's your birthday bumps.'
I didn't yell, just gave him a thump.

I opened my presents with great joy
Then played with my favourite toy.
I couldn't wait for my friends to arrive
Especially John, he got me a beehive.

They finally came, smiles on faces
I sat them down in their places.
I gave them all pop and cake
The one that took hours to bake.

After that it was party games
We all made paper trains.
Then they went, said goodbye
It was over so quick, time does fly.

After that I went to bed
Thinking of what my mum had said.
'Goodnight, have happy dreams.'
But was it as good as it seemed?

Jade Leake (12)
Crofton High School

2003 . . .

We all say we are humane
We say we wouldn't murder
Pointlessly, we took lives
Unknown to us
Not of our own free will
We left mothers without children
Children without family
Wives without husbands
Unbeknown to us . . .
We sent our soldiers
Into a valley of death.
People who are a part of this country
And our flesh and blood
We cried as we saw them on the news
Vanish over the horizon
Wives kissed their husbands for the last time
September 11th -
Screams of pain filled the world
From the bereaved and the dying
Was this the excuse for murder?
Homes shattered and destroyed
Like *Lego* buildings knocked down
By some giddy toddler.
Lives shattered like glass
Lives passed like floating ships in thick fog
Still what was the reason?
What use is it to cry over a grave?
Soldiers' names forgotten like dreams
Dust, gunfire and smoke hung over Iraq
Like a black plague
Children playing in the rubble
Of their grandparents' houses
What have we achieved?
Death, destruction.
Iraq, a lawless country
Our soldiers' lives lost in vain
We did free a country,
But we opened Pandora's box . . .

Isabel Poskett (14)
Crofton High School

The Sun Attacks

The day began like any other,
But ended in a mess,
It all began on a cold winter's day,
When the sun god gave war.

The sun god advanced on Wakefield town,
Intent on wide destruction,
When he entered the townspeople cried,
'Go away we're happy with life.'

First he marched for the plentiful fields,
He burnt and fried the crops,
He left them dry and dead,
But now he wanted lives.

He decided to heat up the cathedral,
So he set off there at once,
He entered the building and turned up the heat,
The people were wet with sweat.

Now he aimed to take on thousands,
Going for the centre.
As he approached the town centre,
A brave man cried, 'To arms, to arms.'

The townspeople armed themselves quickly,
With buckets of water and fans,
They made their stand and stood tall,
Against the king of heat.

A great battle was fought that day,
But the people came out on top.
The battle was done, but so was the damage,
The crops were gone for good.

'We will be ready the next time he comes
And beat the weather down!'

Sam Cotton (12)
Crofton High School

The Weather Wages War On Wakefield

Destructively she shows her power,
Drying out land with her arrows of heat.
Out on the suburbs she turns cunningly evil,
Slowly . . . slowly,
Her cackle of laughter brings bullets of rain.
Wakefield's retail park is lashed with water,
Rising . . . rising,
She smells fear!
She edges in on the crowded town,
Then strikes with torturing daggers of lightning.
Marching away with her army of torture,
She screeches as she hammers the ground.
Occupied with evil,
The fog smothers the sky,
Hail spears the land.
Her sinful behaviour brews more and more vicious
As she drowns her victims,
One by one.
Their security is no longer protective,
Once again she roars with hate
And makes the Devil look harmless.
She brings dark clouds of death,
With knives of ice as sharp as blades.
The silent whisper is broken,
When she cackles with balls of fire.
Never doubt the power of evil,
She is watching you!

Kristy Nestor (12)
Crofton High School

The Violent Volcanic Disaster

Volcanic rock fell violently from the sky,
Walton was raging, people running, shouting,
Houses smashed, roads blocked,
People diving for cover.

Lava came in tons,
Rolling down the hillside,
Burning hot, scorching the fields and roads,
It was getting near, very near.

Fire trucks came screaming, 10, 20, 30,
Made a road block and sprayed the lava,
Steam rose and blinded the onlookers,
Bang, bang, bang! The ground shook,

The 40 foot monster stomping,
His hammer rose and with a mighty force,
The hammer hit the ground and people fell
Fell into the dark abyss.

The fire trucks were holding,
The lava was seeping away,
All the rocks had fallen
And the monster's volcanic reign was ending.

In the morning the clear up had begun,
Steam still rose from the road,
Cranes moved in, bridges were built over the abyss,
The people finished the work at long last.

People became used to the gap
And lives became normal again.

Chris Hoyle (12)
Crofton High School

The Teachers

Teachers are nothing, they just wanna get paid,
Worried about what we're wearin' instead of our grade,
They sure would like to yell at ya fast,
But it's best to get up and walk out of class.
Steady tryin' to teach me compare and contrast,
Sayin' you listen and stay on task.
Man get out of my face,
You think just cos you're a teacher
You ain't got a place.
Let's see you tell me what to do,
When I've got a bigger vocab than you.
You think cos you're a teacher you're smarter than me,
Asking me questions you're the one with the degree,
The teachers had better think twice,
Up in class tryin' to give me advice,
With or without you I'll make it on my own,
Hey let the word be known.
In my eyes I'm already half grown,
I'm making straight 'A's,
I don't need no teacher to show me the ways,
I'm sick and tired of listening to teachers
And waking up in the morning
For another school day.

Danielle Pinnell (13)
Crofton High School

Forest

As I walked through the mist
They all stared at me
They bowed down in curiosity
And looked around to see.

I plodded through the mud
Splish, splosh, I did go
The sun peeked through them
Like a star that sparkled so.

It lit up the forest
Like the brightness of the sunrise
The trees were smiling down at me
As I left I felt I was hypnotised.

Kimberly Grundy (12)
Crofton High School

Shy

When I'm walkin' down da street,
I'm looking at my feet.
There's a car goin' by . . .
'n' I'm feeling kind of shy!
I think to myself, *am I goin' to live or die?*
But I don't wanna say goodbye,
now it's time to cross da road,
but there's some kind of secret code!
1, 2, 3 and off I go.
I can move real quick,
I can move real slow.
I sometimes wonder when people walk by,
what it must be like not to be shy.

Jessica Goldthorpe (13)
Crofton High School

Snake

Stealthy slinker,
Skin shedder,
Silent stalker,
Non walker,
Bone cruncher,
Animal muncher,
Camouflaged creeper,
Full rat eater,
Constricting crusher,
Strong pusher,
Scaly spitter,
Solid hitter,
Acidic rattler,
Venomous battler,
Poisonous biter,
Valiant fighter,
Human thriller,
Species killer!

Jake Rylatt (11)
Crofton High School

Phone

You might have one in a household
You might have one in a car
You might use it near
You might use it afar
You might hear it *ring, ring*
You might hear it *brring, brring*
You might have one bigger
You might have one smaller
It's a colourful caller.

Holly Birkinshaw (11)
Crofton High School

Horse (Galloping)

Mane flower,
Breath blower.

Ground shaker,
Human waker.

Grass trampler,
Plant sampler.

Food guzzler,
Person nuzzler.

Nose flarer,
Bridle wearer.

Stable lover,
Undercover.

Jump springer,
Happy singer.

Sallie Freear (12)
Crofton High School

Orang-Utan

Super swinger,
Banana bringer,
Jungle fighter,
Sleep at nighter,
Clever speaker,
Bit of a reeker,
Stylish swayer,
Nit slayer,
Orange fur grower,
He's up in the trees,
He won't go lower.

Rob Dawson (11)
Crofton High School

The Sun's Assault

Fog clung to the street like toffee on a rug,
As if the clouds had fallen from the sky.
If only the sun would come out today,
Thought many of the villagers standing by!
Suddenly the air turned close and muggy,
And the fog seemed to be slowly slipping away.
Then down came an arrow of blinding light,
And the villagers knew they would have to fight!

Continuous strips of light came down,
As if they'd been shot from a bow.
The fiery daggers stabbed the ground,
So as we were attacked it just went to show,
Be careful what you wish,
Because sometimes the fog is better than the sun!
(If you see what I mean!)
And that was the reason 'this' war had begun!

Laser beams were reflected off every window,
Explosions of light ricocheted off the lake.
The ground was turning a sandy brown,
Which obviously showed it was starting to bake.
Then out of the clouds came her treacherous face,
Staring at us with those fire licked eyes.
While the sun kept us in her villainous gaze,
It got us hoping this was just a weather faze.

At this point I decided to give her some back,
I got an umbrella and put it over my seat.
Many of the others followed my lead,
To keep them protected from the siring heat.
Suddenly I could see the sun started to look worried,
And slowly retreat behind the clouds,
Thank goodness the war had ended.

Becky Ibbotson (12)
Crofton High School

The Woeful War!

Oh why, oh why did this begin?
If it's not our fault, whose is it?
The plants, the animals, the children's or God's?
Anyone's fault but ours.

The rifles rattling about our head,
All came from the enemy first.
That's whose fault it is,
Anyone's fault but ours!

All the people who died out there,
For king, queen and country.
We didn't kill them or did we?
Anyone's fault but ours!

We wish we could start again,
Maybe we're feeling guilty?
We've started to see what's happened here,
Still it's anyone's but ours!

All those protests, what were they for?
The Government? But they don't listen!
But maybe, just maybe, they've started to see,
That maybe it is our fault!

Hang on, what about me?
What about my view?
What about the children's view?
Does anyone actually care?

People my age die every day,
They even fight in war.
But in my world nobody listens,
Nobody tells me why!

I know more about the war,
I watch and listen but don't speak.
I can see that everyone's to blame,
That's just how we are!

Sophie Wiehl (12)
Crofton High School

Batsman

Wicket hater
Duck disliker
Trophy winner
Tone maker
Four smasher
Six lover
Window breaker
Crowd pleaser
Helmet wearer
Big hitter
Run seeker
Ball shaker.

Sam Malyan (11)
Crofton High School

Tiger

Stronger and stronger
Heavier and braver
Slayer
Want to live longer
Rarer and rarer
Prey stalker
Meat muncher
Bones barer
Faster and faster
Paw printer
Fur thicker
Jungle master.

Emily Bullock (12)
Crofton High School

Cat

Creative catcher
Butter eater
Toe biter
Furniture scratcher

Late night yowler
Deafening purrer
Fur ball spitter
Night-time prowler

Sly creeper
Stealthy stalker
Silent pouncer
Deep sleeper

Fish muncher
Mouse finder
Focused hunter
Biscuit cruncher.

Jessica Coates-Bridgewater (11)
Crofton High School

Blackbird

Bread eater
Sky flier
Worm seeker
Berry eater
Window messer
Morning singer
Water bather
Tree rester
Ground strutter
Twig collector
Egg warmer
Baby raiser.

William Hinitt (11)
Crofton High School

Lion

Powerful killer,
Animal hunter,
Prey catcher,
Meat eater.

Evil teether,
Friend hater,
Love creator,
Fur snatcher.

Fast runner,
Bone breaker,
Mean traitor,
Grass hater.

Hannah Morley (11)
Crofton High School

Riddle

Bouncy bums
Waggly tails
Floppy ears
Chirpy chums
Noisy bark
Active pups
High jumpers
Walks in park
Loud calls
Runs fast
Soft paws
Catches ball.

Answer: A dog.

Olivia Ferguson (11)
Crofton High School

Brown Mouse

Twitching whisker,
Cheese nibbler,
Floor scraper,
Life risker.

Hole maker,
Nose twitcher,
Little squeaker,
Risk taker.

Pest scurrier,
Albino eyeballer,
Hairless tailor,
Nest builder.

Toothy nibbler,
Tail wriggler,
Soft pawer,
Under hider.

Chad Banks (11)
Crofton High School

The Dog

Four-legged walker
Bone chewer
Ball chaser
Loud barker

Cat fighter
Fast runner
Food gorger
Hard biter.

Joe Bannister (11)
Crofton High School

Ticking Clock Kenning

Electric user
Time giver
Music player
Slow hand mover

Noise maker
Red hand faster
Black hands slower
Loud waker

Time chaser
Red hand ticker
High walker
Late maker.

Jamie Lee Maclennan (11)
Crofton High School

Death

Like a creeper
Breath stealer
Heart breaker
Leaves a weeper
Life taker
By a murderer
Or some other
Meet your maker
Beat stopper
Body stiller
Body burner
Stiff as copper.

Mandy Arnold (11)
Crofton High School

My Mental Teacher

My teacher has
lost the plot
He's gone completely
mad!
I came in the class
second from last
and I've never seen him
run so fast!
He charged at me with a
rugby
tackle,
he let out a
massive cackle!
Later on in
detention
no one paid any attention
so he picked up
little Jeff Findow and
threw him straight out the
window!
Someone ran for the
door,
he shot him to the floor!
Then he turned around
to give a
lecture,
'Watch out kiddies I'm comin' to get ya!'

Eleanor Armitage (13)
Crofton High School

My Computer

My computer is my best friend,
He always plays with me.
When I'm upset
He tries to comfort me.
When I sing,
He sings along too.
He is there for me
When I'm upset.

My computer was my best friend,
My dad took him away!
What will I do?
No one to play with.
My dad says I was crazy,
But he was my best friend.

Heather Ball (13)
Crofton High School

Football

My poem's about football
It's based around a ball
There's goalkeepers, midfielders, defenders
Who try to get the ball
But the place I would play is not in the wall
I would play attacker
Who scores all the goals
Like Henry, Owen, van Nistelrooy and Sheringham
If he wasn't too old
I would play for Madrid with Beckham, Figo and Raul.

Matthew Raine (13)
Crofton High School

The Value Of Life

Life is so precious,
that's why I'm telling you.

Life is so precious,
you should not forget it.

Life is so precious,
you get a chance, you take it.

Life is so precious,
you won't forget a thing.

Life is so precious,
that's why I'm telling you.

Life is so precious,
you want to write it down.

Life is so precious,
it's like a little gem.

Life is so precious,
it's worth every moment.

Life is so precious,
that's why I'm telling you.

Life is so precious,
you've all got a heart.

Life is so precious,
don't kill it off.

Nathan Hartley (14)
Crofton High School

Pets

I have a dog called Bundle,
He loves to trundle.
His bowl clean he licks,
Then he starts to do tricks.

I have a cat,
Who keeps finding rats.
Guess where?
Under the mats.

I have a parrot,
Who likes carrots.
He talks to me,
Then whacks me.

I have a rabbit,
Who has a very bad habit
Of picking his nose
And then flicking them at me.

I have a hedgehog
Who likes to do tricks
Guess what?
He likes to prick you.

Saad Afzal (13)
Crofton High School

A Bin

Food holder
Rubbish eater
Binman taker
Binbag shoulder

Boneless meaner
Rubbish shaker
Rubbish emptier
Lonely loaner.

Joe Lewis Rodgers (11)
Crofton High School

My Consequences

I stepped into the classroom
and everybody glared,
I knew why they hated me,
I knew why no one cared.

It was my fault, I can't deny,
I made her feel alone.
I taunted her, I laughed at her,
I forced her to stay at home.

I was so evil,
I really can't see,
I can't believe what I've done,
I can't believe it was me!

I wish I could say sorry,
I wanted to say I was sorry,
But I'm never going to see her,
There's no bullies where she's gone!

Hayley Lingard (13)
Crofton High School

Horse

Crowd screamer
Fun maker
Honey shaker

Big jumper
Fast runner
Grass chomper

Mud chucker
Girl bringer
Lady flirter.

The horse is Champ!

Joe Whitehouse (11)
Crofton High School

War

Slaughtered men
Blown up buildings
Smashed windows
Broken bones
Bloody streets
Ripped clothes
Screaming children
Echoes of gunshots
Noisy tanks
The shriek of pain
Bleeding guts
Soldiers running
Cruel assault
Exploding grenades
The mortar crashes
The artillery waits
The guns fire
People killing
People dying
Where is the love?

Lee Brealey (13)
Crofton High School

Mum

As warm as a cup of hot chocolate,
Sometimes cheerful, sometimes sad;
Blazing red hair like a ruby-red flame,
Eyes as misty as a spring sky, which makes you feel
as light as a feather.
A smile which is as contagious as chickenpox,
As trendy as 'Posh', as sleek as a glamorous cat;
She tries to be cool, but it doesn't always work,
Still . . . she is my mum!

Hannah Jones (11)
Crofton High School

No One Cares About Me

As I lie awake cold and alone,
With no place to call my home.

Starving and dying as I lay,
I haven't eaten anything today.

Who cares about me?
To everyone else I'm nobody,
That's all they see.

As they pass me by,
Without a tear in their eye.

Why should they take pity,
When they are rich living in the city?

Maybe one day they too will see,
When they look through the eyes of me.

Sarah Wilkinson (13)
Crofton High School

Parents! What Do They Know?

'You're not going out dressed like that!'
I look down at the floor.
'You've an attitude problem young lady,'
Parents are such a bore.

'Get out of my sight!' they shouted,
I'm only too happy to go.
'Less of the lip young madam,'
Parents - what do they know?

'You're grounded now, get to your room!'
I stand there and just stare.
'Don't answer me back, you cheeky little girl,'
Mum, Dad, I don't care!

Michaela Morgan (14)
Crofton High School

Scared Of Being Dead

When I was young, I was scared of being dead,
I asked, 'Is it black or is it red?
Do I need a penny to get on a boat?
Or does a zombie pull you by the throat?'
Grim Reaper touches your shoulder,
Is it just me or has it got colder?
Dreams of death frightened me loads!
'Would me and my family get reincarnated into toads?
How will I know if I'm dead or not?
Will it be cold or will it be hot?
Does God greet you at Heaven's door?
Or does the devil throw you to a fiery floor?'
But now I don't think of being dead,
Now I have other things in my head!

Alicia Millthorpe (13)
Crofton High School

Old People

Why do old people eat sloppy food?
Why do old people always wear slippers?
Why do old people snore?
Why do old people have their own smell?
Why do old people love gardening?
Why do old people keep your football if it goes in their garden?
Why do old people always moan?
Why do old people feed the ducks?
Why are old people so boring?
Why are old people always cold?
It's probably because they are old.

Tom Broadbent (14)
Crofton High School

My New Best Friend

My new best friend
is tiny and black,
My new best friend
is called Jack.
My new best friend
is from Millwall,
My new best friend
is 8 inches tall.
My new best friend
likes having fun,
My new best friend
loves to run.
My new best friend
eats Pedigree Chum,
My new best friend
has left his mum.
My new best friend
is a bit of a pest,
My new best friend
ate half my vest.
My new best friend
is as good as he could be,
My new best friend
is a cute little puppy.

Greg Hudson (13)
Crofton High School

My Dog

Who barked at Grandma when she walked through the door,
Who scratched the table and chewed up the floor.
Who chased next-door's cat away from the house,
Who ate a dead rat and spat it back out,
Who ran up the stairs and jumped on the bed,
Who left her food and ate the chicken instead.

My dog.

Daniel Turner (11)
Crofton High School

How I Escape

You climb up onto the horse
You can feel its thundering force

It breaks into a canter

You can feel the wind against your face
As it has quickened its pace

I can see the amazing landscape . . .
Breathtaking
For me it is there waiting

It began to run as fast as the speed of light
As it went into a gallop with all its might

It made me feel like I was free
And there are no troubles near me

I felt like a superhero in a cape
As you can tell this is my way to escape.

Francesca Embling (12)
Crofton High School

Hell

A hot burner,
A steaming boiler,
A powerful flamer,
A spreading infecter,
An abysmal painer,
A terrible diseaser,
A killing torturer,
A mean punisher,
It couldn't get crueller,
The home to . . .
Death.

Michael Grantham (11)
Crofton High School

Kitten Gone

Dumped in a river and abandoned
Sinking
Her life flashing before her eyes
Sinking
The sky was black and grey
Sinking
The kitten struggling to get air
Sinking
Pulled under by the ferocious current
Sinking
The water was cold and frosty
Sinking
Unusual fish powerfully swimming by observantly
Sinking
The water was dark yet lively
Sinking
She tried one last break upwards
Then she was gone.

Thomas Mitchell (12)
Crofton High School

Football Poem

The atmosphere makes me cheer
The shouts around the ground ring in my ear
All around the ground you can hear
Excitement as the game gets near.

A player runs and kicks the ball
Past the defender who is very tall
Was he pushed or did he fall?
'Penalty, penalty,' all the crowd call.

Brightly coloured stewards light up the ground
Chanting fans make lots of sound
Music booming, *pound, pound, pound*
Football is the best game ever found.

William Barley (12)
Crofton High School

The Storm

It was a cold, dark night
The wind was blowing
And it was raining heavy
Hailstones bouncing off the floor
Trees swaying from side to side
The sky was cloudy
And as dark as night
The streets were flooding
The drains were blocked
Was I ever going to get home?
The storm was getting worse
It started to thunder
Then lightning struck in front of my eyes
I was scared
I started to run
The thunder was getting louder
It was like it was chasing me
I kept running
I could see my house by now
But would I ever reach it
Or will the storm bring me down?

Jessica Grindle (13)
Crofton High School

Christmas Treat!

Delicate patters on the roof,
the gentle movement of each hoof,
Santa appears so gleeful and merry,
he delivers his presents while swigging his sherry.
The dainty fairy on top of the tree,
the crackling fire with flames so free.
Silvery icicles fall from the sky,
the clouds look sullen, they're way up high.
Kids in wellies pulling a sleigh,
wrapped up in scarves, such a wintry day.

Laura Grinsill (13)
Crofton High School

The Seaside

The bright yellow sun
Shining in the sky
The bright blue sea
Twinkling under it
Beautiful water, coloured shells
Cover the sand
Gorgeous smell of candyfloss
In the air
Mixes with the strong smell of
Fish and chips
Children playing in the beach
People jumping up in the water
Kids splashing and screaming
A great day.

Parveen Hussain (16)
Crofton High School

In Our House

In our house it's loud and cool
There's people dancing like baboons
It's loud then quiet and really good
You have a great laugh in our new house.

In our house it's loud and cool
There's people singing like strangled cats
There's family and friends been really bad
Everybody's the same in our new house.

In our house it's loud and cool
I like to sing in my brand new room
And everybody likes to listen to me
Everyone loves our new house.

Samantha Blakeston (13)
Crofton High School

Animals Of The World

Dogs are fluffy
Rabbits are nice
Snakes are slimy
And cats eat mice

Spiders are scary
Rats are fat
Donkeys are cute
And fish are flat.

Squirrels eat nuts
Kangaroos bounce
All wasps sting
And tigers pounce

Sharks eat seals
Dolphins too
Jellyfish sting
And cows go moo

All the animals in the world
Who live on the land and in the sea
All are different
All are free.

Emma Fenn (13)
Crofton High School

Scar On My Mind

Another scar on my mind,
Left by the image,
An image of a friend,
Another friend gone,
Gone from hell,
I hope I'll soon go,
So I run,
Run until I forget why I run,
Or where I run,
And I fight,
Fight for my life,
An inch from death,
Always an inch from death,
And there goes another,
Another of my friends gone,
Slumps to the ground,
A friend I don't know,
He falls,
But that friend falls by my hand,
We are all friends,
We just don't know each other,
We are all humans,
All friends,
Is it for my country,
Or for their country?
I wish I could live for my country,
Maybe I shall if I get out of this hell,
All I know is I will die today,
Until I wake tomorrow,
Still in my hell.

Josh Stanley (13)
Crofton High School

Summer

The sun is out
That's what summer is about
The lotion is on
And the clouds have gone

Kids are sat on the beach
The volleyball they cannot reach
Barbecues people have had
Because now the weather is getting bad

Everyone is having a cold drink
But the sun will have gone in a blink
The sun is really hot and burning
But at least the kids aren't learning.

Grace Cook (13)
Crofton High School

A Hamster

Bed nester
Wood chewer
Expert scuttler
Easy rester
Daytime sleeper
Easy goer
Local hibernator
Little creeper
Human pleaser
Professional gnawer
Food nibbler
Cat teaser.

Charlotte Upex (11)
Crofton High School

Christmas

Days are so cold
When you get old
Log fire's burning
Bellies are churning.

Christmas is coming
Birds are humming
Presents are being bought
Of every sort.

Night is here
While men drink beer
Children are peeping
When everyone's sleeping.

Snowmen are built
Flowers start to tilt
Hot cocoa is being made
Tiny children are afraid.

Tonight is the night
Everything's looking bright
Santa is near
The whisky will soon disappear.

Marie-Ann Robson (14)
Crofton High School

My Dog

Sofa chewer
Loud shower
Food scoffer
Fast runner

Loud moaner
Big jumper
Ditch digger
Noisy chewer.

Craig Spooner (11)
Crofton High School

People

In this world there's ups and downs,
People happy,
People sad,
People caring,
Always sharing,
Always daring,
Always scaring.
In this world there's peace and war,
People fighting,
People who hide behind the door,
People angry,
People mad,
People sad,
People understanding like they're dads.
In this world there's lots of mates,
People boring,
People who go on dates,
People funny,
Cute as bunnies,
People bright as the weather when it's sunny
And people who love money.
In this world there's lots of children,
People homeless,
People who live in buildings,
People who have lots of money,
People who don't,
People greedy,
And people who can't even afford a coat.

Danielle Arnold (13)
Crofton High School

Darkness

I'm sad and lonely, sitting in the dark,
I daren't turn the light on in case the dog barks.
There's a plane overhead, the engine growls,
The sky's full with smoke, as the siren howls.
I heard a few gunshots, then a few screams,
What if it's my family, no we're a team.
When dodging bombs I see frightened faces,
They struggle along with bags and cases.
The lightning strikes, the gunshots get louder,
Many lives gone like a gust of sweet powder.
The debris has cleared and the planes are gone,
The house is deserted, there's no one . . . no one!
The dog's on the floor, a wound in his chest,
I covered his body and lay him to rest.
I staggered out the cellar, into hell,
My knees went weak and I just fell, fell, fell.
They were my family, dead on the floor,
Covered with innocent blood, oozing with gore.
Its those soldiers, they killed them, they don't care,
I would've killed myself, if I just dare.
I'm sad and lonely sitting in the dark,
Alone in the world, like a swing in the park.

Rachel Stringfellow (13)
Crofton High School

Eyes

Peek-a-boo!
Your mum used to say
Hiding and then appearing again.
But have you ever taken that second to think
That if you were blind - you wouldn't have had that fun?
Seen the colours
Or the sunny days
Even seen your mum or your dad.
Just think about that today.

Amber Nixon (13)
Dixons City Technology College

Emergency Services

Nee-nor, nee-nor!
Flashing lights,
Sirens,
Nee-nor, nee-nor!

Dial 999! Who do they send?
Red engines, breathing apparatus, helmets
Who have they sent?
They go bursting through the flames,
Rescue all they can!
Saving lives, stopping death,
Keeping spirits high!

Nee-nor, nee-nor!
Flashing lights,
Sirens!
Nee-nor, nee-nor!

Dial 999! Who do they send?
Green crosses, medicine boxes.
Oxygen masks,
Who have they sent?
They run to check your pulse.
Feel for a rhythm,
Saving lives, stopping death,
Keeping spirits high!

Nee-nor, nee-nor!
Flashing lights,
Sirens!
Nee-nor, nee-nor!

Dial 999! Who do they send?
Silver handcuffs, black batons,
A full black suit and hat,
They stop crime, keep civilisation,
Lock the villains in jail.
Preserving laws, stopping crime,
Keeping spirits high!

No lights, no sounds,
No helping hands.
Our voices long,
Our saviours gone,
If we don't pay them
Respect!

Laura Ryan (13)
Dixons City Technology College

The Nine Scary Things

As I hear the scream
We look up.
I hear the scream again,
We look up again.
We crush the food,
We crush the fire.
We run, run, run
But they ride, ride and ride.
We hear the scream one more time,
We look up one more time.
We run, run, run until we can't take one more,
But they ride, ride and ride!

We look up,
We see nine scary things.
We cry, cry, cry -
They laugh, laugh, laugh!

Chris Rodger (12)
Dixons City Technology College

Topsy-Turvy Land

Up the stairs on the second shelf
Lives a jack-in-a-box in the shape of an elf.
With the twist of a handle and the sound of the band,
You'll come to Topsy-Turvy Land.

Zooming down the straight and crooked street,
Incredibly slowly indeed.
He went to the greengrocers for plenty o' meat
And came out with a silver lead.

The dog took the man for a run in the fields,
And the dog stroked the man's bald head.
The man stuck right by the Alsatian's heels
With a bone in his mouth, which was red.

The adults in cots in the back of the room
Are shouting as loud as a bomb.
The babies are feeding them with small, plastic spoons,
Wondering where they came from.

If you climb the stairs of the oldest house,
You'll get to the bottom floor.
All the creatures stir, even the mouse.
Over the oldest door.
On the second shelf, lives a box-in-a-jack,
In the shape of an orange goblin.
If you twist the handle and hear the crack
And the band which makes a din.
You'll feel yourself being turned around again and again,
Until eventually you are backwards . . .
Or forwards, if you know what I mean!

Jake White (12)
Dixons City Technology College

Silence

How would we get the message across?
How would we know what was happening?
We wouldn't know what's going on around the world.
It would be like someone has put a black blanket over us.
Not being able to see.
Not being able to hear.
No phone,
We would moan.
No e-mail,
We would fail.
No TV,
We would not see.
Our lives would be changed forever, without communication.
All we'd hear is . . .
Silence.

Bonnie-Alice Bartlett (12)
Dixons City Technology College

Hallowe'en

Children wander about the street
Screaming out, 'Trick or treat?'
Jack-o'-lanterns glow
Candles flicker
Ghouls and ghosts in your ear
Fear and excitement fill your soul
It's the night of the dead or so I'm told
The older children say I'm silly
Dressing up in something glitsy
But my mum tells me I look lovely
And sends me off into the night.

Naomi Lanigan (12)
Dixons City Technology College

Windows

Windows could let us see the world from a room
But instead we are sat here in lots of gloom.

We wouldn't have to sit here in the dark,
Instead we would be able to look at the park.

Windows, windows bring in the light,
Windows, windows how very bright.

Windows could let us see the world,
We could see the leaves as they twirled.

We would be able to see fields of green,
When our teachers are being mean!

Windows, windows bring in the light,
Windows, windows, what a good sight!

Bethany Jane Armstrong (12)
Dixons City Technology College

Summertime All Over Again

In summertime flowers start to grow into bright colours.
In summertime children start to play with all sorts of things.
In summertime birds start to chirp all through the day.
But in the wintertime . . .
Flowers start to close up and die.
Children stay indoors nearly all the time
And the birds fly away to a warmer place.
But when it gets to summer . . .
It starts all over again!

Deepika Patel (12)
Dixons City Technology College

Time

Time is unbeatable
Time is unfair,
Although you cannot see him
He always is there.

He can tick
He can tock,
His identity is shown
In the face of a clock.

He's so powerful
He controls fate,
But you dearly need him
To go at your rate.

You think not of him
You forget him,
But he'll make you pay
Right up to the brim.

Now remember this poem
For you have been forewarned,
Time is powerful
The most powerful of all.

Time is your master
Time is your friend,
Either way you look at it -
You'll need him in the end.

Kasim Hussain (12)
Dixons City Technology College

Football

Football is a magic thing
Where players play and followers sing
Standing up, sitting down
All the chants, go round and round.

Football is a magic thing
Where players play and followers sing
As the ref controls the game
And all the keepers being put to shame.

Football is a magic thing
Where players play and followers sing
As the final whistle blows
The crowd gives off a big cheer or a moan.

Adam Cosheril (13)
Dixons City Technology College

Arrival

UFOs floating in space
Shiny dishes of silver
Some flat, some big and small
Lights flashing brightly in the dark night
The sounds of hovering, fill the sky
A chill grows bigger and colder it comes down.
A shadow casts
The shape draws near like a ghost.
It says something.
Suddenly a car comes, the lights dazzle the unknown creature
It returns to the raft and shoots like a bullet
A glisten of silver was there and then gone.

Jack Singleton (12)
Dixons City Technology College

The Autumn Leaves

T he seed is planted
H eavy rainfall there is
E ach root bursts out of its shell.

A nother day passes
U nder the space, the eye can see
T he bud has shot out and green leaves grow
U nder the space the eye can see are the roots
M aturing immensely
N ever stopping to wait.

L eaves have grown and are beginning to go golden-brown
E ach leaf hovering down towards the ground like a feather
A rriving on the floor, without a single sound
V ery busy wardens brush up the leaves, every day
E ach leaf brushed up, leaving the park looking spotless
S aving the wind a job.

Chinyere Stapleton (12)
Dixons City Technology College

Imagine

Imagine walking down the street with only you
Imagine having no family, only you
Imagine having no friends but only you
Imagine not talking about your problems with only you
Imagine not seeing anybody each day and night with only you
Imagine no one at school, only you
Imagine no one in the whole wide world, only you
Imagine being so lonely with only you.

Donna Harvey (12)
Dixons City Technology College

Money

I woke up one morning
I went downstairs for something to eat
but there was nothing there.
I walked to the shops in my rags
I got some food and went to the counter
and realised I had no money
So next time you go to a shop -
Think and don't take it for granted!

Sally Robson (12)
Dixons City Technology College

So Called Mighty Lord

I ask you why you punish me
with life's forgotten ways?
I ask you why, when I'm happy
I'm sad again in days?
I ask you why you cannot make
the light shine down on me?
I ask you why your mighty powers
we, the people, do not see?

The topic of the conversation is
why do you make us hate?
With your pain and suffering
the world is in a damn right state!

I know you do not seem to care
that the world is dying
Unhappy people everywhere
most people now choose flying
Whilst you're high, the memories die
and- instead, inside your head
you sit and create a perfect place
whilst lying in your bed.

Gema-Opal McDonald (17)
Greenhead College

Blink

Humidity, acidity,
Incarcerate my liberty.
Dance upon my skin
and then attack my very right to be
Who I am - I have no plan
that you could ever understand

Let me go and let me fly . . .

Into blue skies
Thin ice, in a disguise
Starlight,
Fine print in the dark night,
It's alright,
If we try, then we just might
Sit tight,
to reclaim our eyesight.

Richard Scholes (17)
Greenhead College

Boy Mad

People say I'm boy mad
but is that really, really bad?
I haven't got a favourite boy,
I like them all, they give me joy.
I think about them all the time,
at school, at home, they are divine.
Tom, Steve, John, Shawn, Aaron,
Bob, Thorn, Damian, Darren,
Peter, Andrew, Bradley and Paul.
I really, really like them all.
When I'm much older I have one wish
to marry one, a super dish!

Jemma Louise Gidman (16)
Green Meadows School

My Curse

If I could sit upon a star
And see what the world does see
And if the world could stare right back
What it thinks of me?

Would it see the glassy eyes
And the tangent, plastic skin?
Or would it see blond hair, green eyes
Like the sufferers of my sin?

Is this the way the world sees me?
I wish I could sit upon a star and see.

Sheryl Crosland (16)
Huddersfield New College

A Biscuit

A biscuit's a crumbly kind of thing,
It doesn't look sharp and doesn't look neat,
It looks rather soft and it looks rather sweet,
It looks almost like a circular moon.

Nathan Sumpner (11)
John Jamieson School

Porridge

My favourite breakfast,
Porridge with jam and treacle too.
Tastes sweet, like runny honey.
Do you like it too?

Adam Charlesworth (11)
John Jamieson School

Spelling

When I get speling I'm happy
I luv lurning how to spel werds
The teecher tells me to use a computar
The computar tells me the speling is rong
(And they are always rite).
One tyme the computar wrote gobbledegook
I got told off!
(The computar's always rite).
The computar was playing up with my freinds
The same thing was hapening to them
We told the teecher the computar was rong
The teecher told us that
The computar is always right!
The question is -
If the computar is always rite
Why am I speling lyke this?

Claire Thomas (15)
John Jamieson School

Apple

An apple is a kind of fruit,
It doesn't look spiky and it doesn't look cute.
It looks rather round
And it looks rather tasty.
It looks rather like a wheel from my wheelchair.

Jordan Bottomley (13)
John Jamieson School

I Didn't Mean To

I didn't mean to laugh so loud
I made your windows rattle
And your jam jar split in two.

I didn't mean to laugh so loud
I made your best plates scatter
And your picture twisted on the wall.

I didn't mean to laugh so loud
Your budgie flapped against the cage
And the television stopped.

I didn't mean to laugh so loud
The bulbs in your house just went *pop!*

God said that if I didn't change my laugh
He'll banish me from the sky forever.

But what's so wrong . . .
Isn't thunder allowed to laugh?

Salra Mansha (12)
Laisterdyke High School

Falling Leaves

It was the midday
Bright and sunny day
Wind was all around
Leaves flying in the way

Leaves are swinging on the branches
Giving lovely, happy massages
The stormy wind is sweeping the country
Just like a Hollywood actress

You can watch them
And try to catch them
By walls, at corners
But don't forget to play with them.

Hina Rasheed (13)
Laisterdyke High School

Ronaldo's Football Fever

Football crazy.
Ronaldo is mad,
He's been playing football,
Since he was a lad.
On the day of a football match,
Ronaldo took a shot,
Ronaldo hit the post,
And fainted on the spot.
When Ronaldo came off,
He sat on a stool,
The manager came up to him,
And said, 'You stupid fool.'
Ronaldo was a bit upset,
But he wasn't so sad,
The manager said, 'He tried his best,
And he is a big lad.'

Abdul Hassan (13)
Laisterdyke High School

Ya'll Just Don't Understand

Ya'll just don't understand
Football is not just a game to me;
It is a way of life!
The blood, the sweat and the tears
All shed in the name of football.
And my question to you is -
If it were just a game, would we sacrifice so much?
Football is *war* to me!
You lose and your pride is severed.
Your heart is defeated.
I pour my heart and soul into it.
And to lose . . . I think not!
But to you, it's just a game
But then again
Ya'll just don't understand.

Nicholas Hall (12)
Laisterdyke High School

The Story Of Abdul Khan

My home country is Iraq,
And my name is Abdul Khan.
One day my uncle called me,
All the way from Pakistan.

He told us to leave our country,
And I asked him simply, 'Why?'
He told us war was coming,
But my mum said this was a lie.

Later I learned that this was true,
And that our lives were at stake!
So we all fled towards Baghdad,
And took what we all could take.

When we reached the city of Baghdad,
All we saw were vacant rooms.
So we all bunked down in an old house,
But next came all the doom.

Then the British troops came marching,
And hiding we did try.
They approached me with their guns,
And told me I was safe?

Then I heard my mother cry,
All I remember was a shape.
There was blood over here and blood over there,
And blood was all around.

The troops all stood upright and tall,
As if they were all hungry hounds.
But there lay the body of a young soldier,
An innocent boy he lay.

That's when I saw what war had brought,
Only death after death, every day.

Naheem Zafar (13)
Laisterdyke High School

The Ways Of The World

Anyone in the world can be a sufferer
Anyone can be the cause
All it takes is one possible person
To pull the trigger and make everything pause

Already there have been situations
Where people have been left cold, critically wounded or even dead
All it takes is one possible person
To leave everyone else in the red

It can be done through various evil measures
Shooting, bombing, all which is meant
To destroy the people, their livelihood and their homes
And demolish the hopeful internal strength

Based on religion, hatred and anger
It always leads to one thing, innocent civilians who die
All it takes is one possible person
To make the whole world cry.

The correct term for this is terrorism
Every country in the whole world is under threat
It's done by people who have no care
But anger, evil and no regret
The worst cost - leads to death
To those who don't deserve to die
And every day death is reserved and
Could be reversed!

Thawhid Khan (13)
Laisterdyke High School

My Dream

The world is so sweet
so round, so petite.
We all live together
no matter what race or gender.
People happy and enjoying their lives,
no noise, no fighting, no husbands
beating their wives.
No children with tears in their eyes.
everyone goes out freely with no fears,
But this is just my dream when I wake -
there are only tears.
No happy world, no happy faces,
everyone's fighting, even with their own races.
War and poverty, babies dying,
People dead, lost or crying.
What's happened to us, who are we?
I don't want to feel scared or afraid.
We are all human, all God made.
Why can't we just have peace and
appreciate life a bit more?
Forget about these arguments, fighting and war.
We can all try to put things right
and I'll pray for this, until it happens,
every single day and night.

Rabia Mukhtar (13)
Laisterdyke High School

Dream Diary

On Wednesday, I dreamt a giant
who stuck his head
through the classroom window
grabbed her from the desk
and carried *her* off for tea.

On Thursday, I dreamt a pirate
who kidnapped *her*
on *her* way to school
tied *her* up with a rope
and made *her* walk the plank.

On Friday, I dreamt a wizard
who cast a spell on *her*
as *she* barged to the front of the dinner queue
he turned *her* into a rotten banana
and dropped *her* into the bin.

On Saturday, I dreamt an alien
that landed its spacecraft on the roof of the hall
dragged *her* out of assembly
and kept *her* prisoner forever.

On Sunday, I dreamt a ghost
that haunted *her* bedroom
waking *her* up with blood-curdling screams
that made *her* teeth chatter
and *her* hair turned white.

But on Monday there I saw
her and *her* gang
waiting for me
as usual
by the school gates.

Samayya Afzal (12)
Laisterdyke High School

Think

Think of the future
Don't live in the past
Think of what this life is worth
And try and make it last.

Think of the birds
Singing as they fly
Think of this Earth
With its clear blue sky.

Think of the wind
As it blows sins away
Being a good person
Will get you through the day.

Think of the starving
How their lives are with strife
Spare them a thought
And you'll live a happy life.

Forget all the anger
And quarrels you may bear
Because in this life
You must learn to share.

So think of the future
Don't live in the past
This life is beautiful
So enjoy it while it lasts!

Aishah Hamid (13)
Laisterdyke High School

I'm Frustrated

I woke up in the morning,
Brother thumped me on the head,
'I'm frustrated!' I groaned.

Eating breakfast,
Brother swore at me,
I swore back,
Dad told *me* off!
'I'm frustrated!' I moaned.

Playing in the garden,
Fell off my bike,
Brother laughed at me,
I gave him dirties
Dad told *me* off!
'I'm frustrated!' I mumbled.

Eating lunch,
Brother kicked me under the table,
I kicked him back,
Dad told *me* off!
'I'm frustrated!' I muttered.

Watching telly,
Brother got in the way,
I told him to move,
He told Dad,
Dad said, 'Go to bed!'
'I'm frustrated,' I argued.

Adeeb Ashfaq (12)
Laisterdyke High School

School

School is very boring,
Waking up early in the morning.

Going to school five times a week,
And what are teachers? Weird geeks.

Having English, maths and art,
What do they think we are? *Smart!*

In PE we are playing tennis,
And our teacher is called Dennis.

Our caretaker is very big,
You'll always see him with a cig.

Then there is the head,
His name is Fred.

I am in Year 2,
My teacher is called Mrs Loo.

Finally comes the break,
Next year we have got Mr Drake.

Mohammed Waqas Khan (12)
Laisterdyke High School

One Fine Day

One find day in the middle of the night
My mum said, 'Good morning,'
My dad said, 'Goodnight!'
My brother said, 'You're silly!'
While bouncing on his head
And my little baby sister just won't go to bed
And this is meant to be a normal family!
Well do me a favour . . .
Don't include *me!*

Danielle Kenehan (13)
Laisterdyke High School

NFL

Time slows down
As the pass slips from his fingers
Monstrous blockers attack from all sides
Like rampaging rhinos
So fast that movement blurred
The ball left his hand
The wide receiver was waiting for the catch
As the ball floated through the air
The crowd was still not making a sound
As the ball spun round and round
The crowd screamed as the wide receiver, Rod Smith
Turned and caught it
A side-step past one man
He sped straight past another
The line, twenty feet away now, he glanced behind
Him to see the defenders trailing
Behind him
He was running like a flowing river
It didn't stop
And the crowd went wild as the ball went over the line.

Touchdown Broncos

Nathan Dickinson (13)
Pudsey Grangefield School

Homework Blues

I'm sick a' doin' homework
There's not enough time in the day
By the time I hav' dun' it all
There's no time left to play

I wish there wasn't homework
I wish I had more time
Then at least when school did end
The evening would be mine!

Peter Mitchell (12)
Pudsey Grangefield School

School!

I go to school to learn and play
In art I like making things with clay
I come to school nearly every day
The rules we have to obey.

Our school is quite cool
It would be better with a pool.

I think PE is ace
I always come out with a red face
I think science is boring
I could fall asleep and start snoring.

I think Mr Mars is great
He talks to you like he's your mate.

I like my school
As I've said, it's quite cool.

Lewis Bowers (12)
Pudsey Grangefield School

Life

Life is full of dreams,
nothing is what it seems.

You have to work hard,
to earn your wages.

To earn your respect,
down through the ages.

So don't live your life,
cooped up in cages.

So get out and about,
and live life at its full.

Life is full of dreams,
nothing is what it seems.

Jenny Day (12)
Pudsey Grangefield School

The Seasons

S pring is the dawn of all flowers
P ansies
R oses
I n every colour
aN d every size
The G reat outdoors is back again.

The S un is here!
U mbrellas are gone!
M any people are away
But M any stay at home
E very year we enjoy it the most
R ight to the very end.

A nd then comes autumn
U mbrellas back out everyone!
T he weather is cold again
YoU wrap up warm
M ake sure you're warm!
N ever turn off the heating!

The W ind whips across your face
I n comes the snow
N ever giving up in snowball fights
T here are snowmen *everywhere!*
E very year these are the seasons . . .
R ound and around!

Jennifer Whittam (12)
Pudsey Grangefield School

The Leopard

The leopard leaps from tree to tree,
She smoothly claws the ground,
Her cubs are prancing gracefully,
Rolling all around.

She gazes on a passing antelope,
Alone on the dusty plains,
Then stalks her prey till it loses hope,
Then pounces on the lonely game.

The leopard leaps from tree to tree,
She smoothly claws the ground,
Her cubs are gnawing happily,
On the feast that they have found.

Daniel Styran (12)
Pudsey Grangefield School

Television

Television,
A mighty colour screen,
Like the heavens above the clouds.

Television,
1950's black and white to
1970's colour,
The dominant object in the house.

Television,
A child's obsession,
A man-made object.

Television,
Flashy and gaudy,
A new entertainment system for kids.

Tom Yearby (12)
Pudsey Grangefield School

Elephants!

Some people think that elephants are just clumsy and almighty.
But most people know that they are just ravishing creatures hoping
to get through life without being hunted down.
When they take their gigantic strides, they make the Earth shake.
Don't confuse it with an earthquake.
Their grand ears just flopping from side to side.
Their mammoth trunks drooping to the ground.
Hunters want their magnificent white tusks as their own.
The adventurous creatures taking proud, elegant strides
across the Earth's terrain.
The baby holds onto its mother, walking away into the sunset.

Amelia Milnes (13)
Pudsey Grangefield School

The Climb

I looked up at this ancient cliff,
I've heard it's from the Ice Age,
It towers above all the trees,
Above, birds flew in the sky,
I can't explain how petrified I was,
As I began my ascent up this awesome,
Face of rock . . .

I look down now and wonder why,
I was ever scared of climbing this wondrous cliff,
This monstrous, fantastic natural wonder,
Now I want to do it all again.

Laura Marshall (12)
Pudsey Grangefield School

The Vampire's Castle

At the creepy dead of night,
In the dingy, dark castle,
A woman is sleeping still,
She must only be in her twenties.

She didn't know the danger she was in,
As the monstrous vampire approached,
The vampire crept up the spiral stairs,
The stairs twirled and curled.

Getting closer and closer up the stairs,
Nearer to the young, thin woman,
At nearly midnight the vampire was hungry,
The pretty woman tossed and turned.

The horrid vampire crept through the door,
As the woman started to stir,
The vampire stopped dead,
Then there was a deafening scream.

The landlord ran up the spiralling stairs,
When he got there to his shock,
She was lying there, bleeding,
She had been attacked by the bloodthirsty vampire . . .

Gareth Clough (13)
Pudsey Grangefield School

Dolphins

Dolphins are like . . .
A shimmer floating through the dark, glassy ocean
A glistening bauble on a Christmas tree
A friend to talk to when you need them
A sleek shadow gliding through calm water
An intelligent person always knowing what to do and where to go
An enormous muscle swishing to and fro in the sea
Bars of silver and blue zooming through a pitch-black tunnel.

Chloë Orbell (12)
Pudsey Grangefield School

Hallowe'en

All the things I put into a potion
To make a sweet and scented lotion.

A cat's claw, a lion's roar,
A pig's tail, a head so frail.
A dog's jaw, a leg or a boar,
A lamb's ear, a human tear.
A toad's tongue, a mouse so young,
An alien's hand, a beach's sand.
A child's tooth, a witch on the roof,
A frog's set of teeth, the land beneath.
Some witch's hair, a man so bare,
A pig's back, Santa's sack.
A tiger's cut, a sheep's gut,
A glass eye, that's the end of my poem, goodbye!

Jamie Delaney (12)
Pudsey Grangefield School

The Magician

The magician knows every trick in the book
He can make things vanish with only one look
He can throw a card up in the air
It does not come down because it's not even there
Handkerchiefs fly from his trouser pocket
And up into the air just like a rocket
He takes some cards out of a packet
Right then the audience makes a racket

He puts his top hat on the top of his head
'Pick a card, any card,' he says
The volunteer picks a card
And looks at it hard
He gives it back to the magician,
The magician puts it back into the pack
It disappears and never comes back.

Paul Bond (12)
Pudsey Grangefield School

The Three Little Pigs

You wouldn't believe what happened to me,
A wolf wanted to eat me for his tea,
He came round my house,
And huffed and puffed,
So I told him to get lost and get stuffed.

So then he went off to my brother's,
My brother said, 'Can't you eat one of the others?'
My brother's house was only made of straw,
So he didn't last long and we all said, 'Awww!'

The wolf wasn't full so he went for my sister,
She said when he blew it was like a twister,
My sister's house was only made of twigs,
So the wolf had now eaten two fat pigs.

The last little pig was, who else but me,
So the wolf came round going, 'Hee, hee, hee!
I've eaten your brother and your sister too,
And now it's time to eat you.'

'No you won't cos my house is well good,
It isn't made from straw or wood,
You must be really stupid and really thick,
If you think you can blow down a house of brick.'

My brother and sister are dead and buried,
Just in case you were getting worried,
So that's the story and I survived,
Unlike the other two who both died.

Jamie Carrington (12)
Pudsey Grangefield School

Dancing

Dancing
Is a part of me,
It stays there in my soul,
I know it's the very heart of me,
Without it there's a gaping hole.

Leaping,
Running,
Twirling,
Hurling,
Expressing all my feelings,
People think it's just moving,
But really there's a meaning.

When I dance it's like someone's lit a fire in me,
I feel I can fly as my adrenaline's rushing twenty to the dozen.

I just give it my all,
Stand proud and tall,
And hear the audience call,
I know that I've done well.

I get lost in the music,
It's like another world,
I wish I could stay forever,
Not go home,
Never,
Never.

Amie Bennett (12)
Pudsey Grangefield School

The House

The house sat on top of the hill
All was quiet and all was still

The windows were smashed and bare
No glam in this house anywhere

A garden lay overgrown
Neglected, I stood alone

Looking at that terrible place

The path walked you to the house
And on the way I saw a mouse

The door had gaps and was all bare
As I looked the door stood and seemed to stare

The paint of the door was scratched and scraped
And the letter box looked and gaped

The bricks on the roof were old and dusty
The old chimney was old and rusty.

Anilah Choudry (12)
Pudsey Grangefield School

A Cold Winter's Day!

Houses nestle under a white blanket of snow,
The town lies peaceful, glistening in the moonlight.

Children's lives are filled with happiness,
As they run through the white, soft, crunchy snow.

Outside, streetlights like a candle glow,
Cars leaving tracks that will leave the snow soft no more.

Buildings are lit and covered in snow,
Looks like a scene from a Christmas card.

Kim J Farrar (12)
Pudsey Grangefield School

The Darkness

At night is when this creature stalks,
It creeps, it sneaks, it crawls and walks.
Corrupt, ungodly, it seeks its prey.
Daylight, its food has got away.
Until tonight it's safe and sound,
But when night falls its fate is bound.
An eternal capture of torture and doom,
It strikes out in the midnight gloom.
A creature of pure malevolence,
Its fog continues to grow more dense.
The wrath of a tiger, the bite of a bark.
The shot of a poacher, the tooth of a shark.
A raven's wing, a siren's call,
A vampire's curse, a graffitied wall.
The black entity mocks in the night,
The eyes of the Devil regain their sight.
Upon the earth's now shattered souls,
They feed the Devil until he is whole.

Arron Richmond (12)
Pudsey Grangefield School

Blue Whale

The blue whale, graceful as can be,
Sleek and shiny, soaring through the deep blue sea,
Peaceful, gentle, intelligent too,
The blue whale does no harm to you,
Yet out in that sea so blue,
Are men on boats searching for you,
Ready to kill,
And drag you home and cut you up down to the bone,
They have no conscience to be so cruel,
When as God's creature you should be free to rule.

Lauren Stevens (12)
Pudsey Grangefield School

The Darkness Is . . .

An endless pit
A dense, black forest
A hungry predator waiting to pounce on me
A hidden danger
A cold, black monster
A silhouette of daylight's sky
A dark, misty sea
A scary tunnel
A murderous carnivore ready to devour me
A huge blackboard
An unpredictable nightmare
A basket holding secrets best left untouched
A vast, mysterious figure
An overpowering feeling
An evil, mechanical robot searching for me
A dramatic scene
A lonely person
An immense blanket smothering all my senses.

Esta Owen (12)
Pudsey Grangefield School

Animal Haikus

You graceful dolphins
In the glimmering sea, killed
By fishing trawlers.

Tigers, striped, wild cats
Beautiful gold and black fur
Why are you dying?

Mighty elephants
Hunted for your ivory
Fragile, precious tusks.

Catherine Foote (13)
Pudsey Grangefield School

Dear Mr Roald Dahl

Dear Mr Roald Dahl,

> I read your poem the other day,
> Whilst in my cosy bed I lay,

You know the one about the TV sets,
How you thought they were an evil pet,

> My mum read the poem too,
> And she totally agrees with you,

I don't mean to sigh or whinge,
Or sob, whine, complain or cringe,

> I regret to say because of you,
> This is what my mum did do,

She got hold of all the TV sets,
In our house that we did get,

> She put them in the boot of the car,
> And then went inside to wear her scarf,

She took the TVs to the charity shop,
I started crying, 'Mum, just stop.'

> But no, she wasn't having it,
> Not one little, tiny bit,

She handed them over to the till,
And got handed back a big, shiny bill,

> Next we went to the bookstore,
> Where she bought a dozen books or more,

Now up till this very day,
I'm really very unhappy to say,

> We put up bookshelves made of wood,
> Where the TV sets had once gracefully stood.

Ayesha Siddiq (12)
Pudsey Grangefield School

TV Heaven

Why do you taunt us so?
Trying to ruin our steady flow,
Telling mums TVs are bad,
That makes us all very sad,
TV is imagination filler,
Not a mind killer,
Although a book is really great,
TV is something you can watch with your mate,
Watching figures move across the screen,
Ghost movies for the teens,
Little kids have cartoons,
Messing about like little loons,
It gives you the latest news,
Mostly with great views,
An advertising heaven,
When you watch channel seven.

Jenny Quarmby (12)
Pudsey Grangefield School

What Am I?

What am I?
I live on a farm,
I won't do you any harm.
I'll do anything for grass,
But I'll give jumping a pass.
I adore my hooves,
I'll never climb on roofs.
I like to trot and canter,
What am I?
I am strong and bold,
I can lift a ton of gold.
I'm scared of bats,
And I don't like cats.
What am I?
I'm a horse of course!

Bobbie Hancock (12)
Pudsey Grangefield School

Hallowe'en!

While walking late at night,
I met an aged crone,
Her clothes were nothing more than rags,
But she sat on a jewelled throne!
I looked at her in my still position,
And I was so scared,
So I used my imaginative vision,
That I ended up going in pairs!
I asked her a lot of questions,
And she got a terrible shock,
So I persuaded to threaten,
So she threatened to put a stop!
'How do you keep your teeth so green
Whilst mine are always white?
Although I rub them vigorously,
With cool, cold slime every night!
Your eyes have such a lovely shade,
A wonderful tone of blue,
That when I look into my magical pot,
It looks just like you!
I've failed so many times to have bad breath,
After eating sewage raw,
Look at your neat nails,
Whereas look at mine,
I use them to strip paint from a door!'
'My dear, there is no secret behind it,
Now I don't mean to brag,
The natural thing you see in front of you,
Well, what I mean is that I'm only a wicked hag!'

Rupali Sharma (12)
Pudsey Grangefield School

Football

The whistle blows to start the game,
The crowd are shouting the whole team's name,
The stadium's an enormous height,
Look, already there's a fight,
The ref comes over to sort it out,
As someone got a banging clout,
The free kick goes to the other team,
All the crowd start to scream,
An excellent shot goes in the net,
Must have been a George Kaddett,
1-0 up at late half-time,
Both the teams each have a lime,
Out they go for the second half,
They look warmer than a scarf,
The whistle blows once again,
Five minutes in and there's a pen,
The keeper looking scared and glum,
He was acting very dumb,
Hits the ball with all his might,
Breaks the net with a great strike,
1-1 with 5 minutes to go,
Edge of the box, his boot starts to glow,
Smacks the ball like a bullet,
Did a lot better than Ruud Gullit,
What a goal, what a goal, 2-1,
Whistle blows, full-time, we won.

Jake Town (13)
Pudsey Grangefield School

Lucky Star!

Shooting star
You were my lucky star
I wished upon you
So many times

If this is what it comes to
Both of us counting those happy days
Eternal happy days
We ever had together

You were my ray of sunshine
I thought I was your lucky star
Then the love died
Cos you'd deceived me

I realise now
That you're a dying star
Your light's disappeared
You're gone from my life.

Fern Pullan (13)
Pudsey Grangefield School

My Life

Willowby, my beloved dead dog
A year ago he died
Tetley also passed away
How I cried and cried.

I feel ill nearly every day
The TV is my best friend
Homework's all I seem to do
Everything needs one big mend

Christmas, the main fighting point
For a boxing match or two
My auntie in the left corner
The other corner, I wonder who?

Melissa Sahin (13)
Pudsey Grangefield School

Death's Drawl

I wish the world
Could be a book
Filled with magic
Betrayal and sin.

Necromancers rule
And heroes fight
To stop the evil
That is their plight.

A happy ending
To meet us last
But far does it seem
For the truth doth bloom.

The human race
Is the sin
And betrayal is
Its hateful game.

The rulers' leaders
Damned them all
Advocates to
The Devil's call.

If none should fight them
Pestilence, famine
War and death
Will take the final ride.

And Metatron with
His iron book shall judge
The apocalypse will
Bear Earth's end.

Dawn Wood (13)
Pudsey Grangefield School

World Of War

Overseas in Iraq,
The war is finished,
Some soldiers are back.
Children were crying,
As they witnessed
Their families dying.
From the explosion of a bomb
Houses were destroyed,
Families were gone.
It shouldn't have taken long,
But it took longer than expected
Until Saddam was gone.
All families will miss
The people they have lost
And now they can only reminisce.
Children are hoping there'll be no more pain,
No more loss,
And no wars again.
Children are crying no more
Now the pain is gone,
And the war.

Holly Bland (13)
Pudsey Grangefield School

My Dream

I had a dream . . .
Of world peace
No more war
A place where there is no more violence
A place where you have no limits
A place where you can live your life to the full
A place where you can defy the laws of gravity
A place where . . . you can be free.

Hannah Rudge (12)
Pudsey Grangefield School

Animals Are For Life

A nimals are for life
N ot for a day
I magine you're an animal
M aybe you want to be treated right?
A nimals are cute
L oving and kind
S afe in your home

A nd loved by you
R espected and trusted
E ver loving

F urry and spiky
O r big and small
R abbits and dogs

L oud and quiet
I n your home
F orever and
E ternity.

Hafsa Naz (13)
Pudsey Grangefield School

September 11

It was a dreadful time,
September 11th,
A sad time as well,
A lot of people were distraught.
Businesses, homes, local shops
Were destroyed.
Hearts were broken,
Members of family rallied round to help.
It was a tragedy.
September 11th.

Laura Shearon (12)
Pudsey Grangefield School

The Darkness

The darkness of midnight rolls upon us,
The moonlight shines through the clouds,
The swaying of the trees,
In the midnight breeze,
Foxes rustle through bags,
The howling of the wind,
Breaks the silence of the night,
The darkness of midnight.

Shadows appear on the walls,
Trees sway to and fro,
Rustling of the autumn leaves,
Crisp is the winter's frost,
All alone I stroll down the street,
I feel so isolated,
I don't know why,
Will anyone ever save me?

Gemma Hughes (13)
Pudsey Grangefield School

That Dream

That dream I had last night,
It gave me such a fright,
It was so different to the dreams I normally have,
It was dark around me,
It was like nothing was in my dream,
It was just blank,
Like it had been erased,
I stepped forward,
And I fell,
Fell deep down,
Until I woke up in my bed.

Sam Benson (12)
Pudsey Grangefield School

The Scalding Desert

I don't know how long I've been in this desert
Slowly dying
No food
No water
The heat is unbearable
The sand so hard to walk on
What's that in the distance?
An oasis
But my hands go straight through
A mirage

I might be stuck for a very long time
I climb over some rocks and see a little spring
It's not a mirage so I follow it
I was saved, the river led to a village.

Jake Wilson (13)
Pudsey Grangefield School

Chocs!

I can't resist these lovely chocs,
Lucky me, there's 5 in a box.
First come caramel, smooth and runny,
That's my favourite, I'm a happy bunny!
Second there's truffle, with a glorious taste,
As I chomp it down, there's none gone to waste.
Third there's white, smooth and creamy,
It feels like Heaven, I must be dreaming!
Fourth there's nut, how I must chew,
I couldn't eat many, only a few!
Lastly there's dark, it seems so strong,
Dear me, it didn't last long!
Oh poor dear me, I've run out of chocs,
I'll have to nip out for another box!

Melanie Knowles (13)
Pudsey Grangefield School

Who's That Stranger?

Your thoughts are happy,
Sitting high in your chair,
But when it comes to others
I guess you just don't care.
I can see an old man
Walking alone in the street,
With cuts on his hands
And no shoes on his feet.
You've got your family
To hug and to hold,
While he has no one to love,
All alone in the cold.
You're laying in your bed,
All warm in the night,
While he's laying in a box
Full of fear and fright.

People look and turn their faces
And think it's not a problem,
But all he wants is a little change
To get him through the day,
Why can't people give him
A little money along the way?

One day you meet him
And he asks for some change,
Of course you deny,
Just don't feel the shame.
But one day you're sorry,
So you go back to see,
But that man you ignored,
Can no longer be.

Corrie McCambridge (12)
Pudsey Grangefield School

Dream

I had a dream about the
World being different
From war-making and peace-loving
But a balance, so can we make it?

We can pull together
To make the world last forever,
Make it brighter.

It wouldn't be so hard
If cut down on crime
To be honest it's about time
We can do it!

We can pull together
To make our world last forever,
Make it brighter.

So get our act together
Before it's too late
And we turn love into hate
Before it's too late.

Darren Scotter (12)
Pudsey Grangefield School

Blue Sea

As calm as a sleeping cat,
It can be sometimes.
As rough as a charging bull,
It can be sometimes.
Consuming wayward vessels
Like a raging monster,
Like an underwater city
Full of brightly coloured sweets,
A roaring white horse,
Galloping towards the land.

Holly Davies (13)
Pudsey Grangefield School

9/11

On the ninth hour
Of the eleventh day
Of the ninth month
Unknown to them
People's lives would change forever
They lived their lives like normal
Until this day came around
In the planes and in the offices
They did their daily things
Until the ninth hour
Of the eleventh day of September
When tragedy struck!
As New York stopped
All heads turned to watch
The towers crumble
Screams could be heard
But nothing could be done
The picture flashed across the world
As the streets of New York filled
The firemen tried their best
People gathered in the streets
Trying to find their loved ones
The eleventh day of the ninth month

Will never be forgotten.

Richard Scott (13)
Pudsey Grangefield School

The Graveyard

In the graveyard late at night
Gravestones lit up by the moonlight
Eerie shadows moving in the dark
Wolves with their blood-curdling barks
The wind was howling in the air
This graveyard is enough to give you a scare.

Steven Pilling (13)
Pudsey Grangefield School

September 11th

The day was fine,
Aeroplanes were flying,
Then one hit one of the Twin Towers,
Thousands were dead,
Then another aeroplane crashed into the Twin Tower,
Thousands more were dead,
At 11 o'clock people were shocked,
People were hurt, devastated.

Fire engines were heard coming,
They tried to get people out,
But they were gone,
All of a sudden the Twin Towers fell down,
More people dead,
Fire engines crushed,
Cars crushed,
Roads blocked,
The Pentagon partly knocked down,
Families searching, looking for their loved ones,
Four days later, still looking for people,
Some were dead, some survived,
Cleaning it up after,
Building the Pentagon back up,
Building more buildings,
Two years to do it,
They're all happier now.

Rebecca Ives (12)
Pudsey Grangefield School

Mirror, Mirror

Mirror, mirror on my bedroom wall,
Why am I so very small?
My ears stick out,
My hair is so thin,
Look at my dreary skin,
I hate my eyes and my smile,
My nails could use a real good file,
I wish I was free instead of trapped under this mess,
It does nothing for me, just makes me stress.
Mirror, mirror on my wall,
Make me beautiful,
Make me tall,
Make me so every eye can see,
What I've become,
What I can be,
But who is that girl in the mirror I see . . . ?
It's not me.

Emma Pritchard (12)
Pudsey Grangefield School

Netball

Netball is a sport I play
Practically every day
If we do not have a match
We practise how to throw and catch
The netball is hard and round
And when you throw it, it hits the ground
The netball posts are long and steep
And when you shoot you have to leap
When you play there's seven positions
Every match is a competition
Goal position and attack are shooters
They have to have minds like computers
Netball is a sport I play
Practically every day.

Kim Terry (13)
Pudsey Grangefield School

A World Where No One Cares

When I woke up one Monday morning,
Some lads were throwing some rocks through my window,
I didn't care, neither did they.
When I went down to breakfast,
Mum shouted at me for no reason,
I didn't care, neither did she.
When I got into the car, I turned on the radio,
The man said he hated everybody,
I didn't care, neither did he.
When I got out of the car,
I saw some people graffiti the school walls,
I didn't care, neither did they.
When I walked into class,
Mr Bentally was sitting there, drinking and swearing,
I didn't care, neither did he.
When we did our experiment in science,
Mr Dole poured toxic acid on our skin,
I didn't care, neither did he.
When I went to lunch,
Some Year 7s were smoking,
I didn't care, neither did they.
When I went to form,
I saw my girlfriend kissing another lad,
I didn't care, neither did she.
When I walked home,
I saw some Year 10s beating up a Year 2,
I didn't care, neither did they.
When I got home,
My mum said, 'I love you Son.'
I finally knew someone who cared,
In a world where no one cares.

Jonathan Nichols (12)
Pudsey Grangefield School

The Year Goes Quick

The year has gone
Really, really quick
All year through
Click, click, click
Easter in the middle
Christmas at the end
It is nearly here
Buying for all your friends
Christmas is really
Really fun
Hope you enjoy it
Run, run, run
Open all your presents
Hurry, hurry, hurry
What have you got?
Cards with lots of money
I love Christmas
Don't you?

Catherine Earl (12)
Pudsey Grangefield School

Football

F eeling the wind on my face
O n the pitch
O n the best team
T he crowd cheering, hear them roar
B all at my feet
A ll my team are calling for it
L ook up and in a flash
L obbed the keeper. Yeah! We won!

Daniel Fretwell (13)
Pudsey Grangefield School

Lady In Light

When I see her I start to melt
If only she knew how I felt
I think about her day and night
She is the lady in the light
When it is cold through the weeks
She puts some colour back into my cheeks
She is as precious as silver, no gold
Nothing about her is dull or bold
Her lips are soft and as red as a rose
She wears colourful and stylish clothes
When she is tired she goes for a rest
I love her like a robin loves its red chest
When they lay their eyes upon her
They start to whisper and begin to ponder
Is this girl walking down the street
A queen, a princess I'd like to meet?
She floats along like on cloud nine
Oh how I wish she would be mine
She's more beautiful than a peacock's feather
I love her like a flower loves the weather
When people see her they drop their cans
In the light this lady stands
Like the wind to a kite
She is the lady in the light.

Kristian Parker (13)
Pudsey Grangefield School

The Big Rock In Space

The big rock in space is a horrible place,
It's full of grime and pollution.
The big rock in space is a horrible place,
It used to be so nice.
The big rock in space is a horrible place,
It's full of cheats and liars.
The big rock in space is a horrible place,
It's full of death and war.
The big rock in space is a horrible place,
It was nice until they got there.
The big rock in space is a horrible place,
They'll kill till nothing is left.
The big rock in space is a horrible place,
But what horrible creatures live there?
The big rock in space . . . is Earth!

James Dawson (12)
Pudsey Grangefield School

Drip, Drop, Drip

The rain pours outside,
From the grey, cloudy sky,
All the animals run to hide,
From the leaky tap in the sky.

Then all in a flash,
The sun peeps through,
And spreads like a rash,
Showing the sparkly dew.

Up above the sun shines,
Like a ball of burning fire,
Reflecting light in golden lines,
Lighting the world from way up high.

Sophie Hood (12)
Pudsey Grangefield School

You Can Choose Your Friends But You Can't Choose Your Family

You can have strange friends, like aeroplanes,
Taking off when you need them most.
But as usual they always come back for you.
You can't choose your family but
You can choose your friends.
Best buds are brill, they'll stay
With you no matter what.
They'll rescue you when you're drifting away
In an ocean of sadness.
You can't choose your family
But you can choose your friends.
Families are fantastic because arguing
Brings you closer in anything, makes your love stronger.
You can't choose your family but you can choose your friends,
When tears are shed and words are screamed, but not meant.
You can count on your family to save you from foolishness.
You can't choose your family but you can choose your friends.
So choose wisely.

Lizzie Pickavance (13)
Pudsey Grangefield School

The Planet

Like a planet
So smooth, shiny and green
A tree growing out of the top
The inside so different
Bumpy and lumpy
Pale yellow all in sight
Nowhere to go
Enormous brown mountains
Stacked up in fours
The only thing different
I know nothing of this planet.

James Barratt (13)
Pudsey Grangefield School

Animals For Life

A nimals are for life,
N ot just to be bought and beaten up,
I will not forgive anyone who does cruelty to them,
M ost people do love their animals,
A nd many people don't,
L ike every person, they have feelings,
S o don't do cruelty to animals.

F rightened for life,
O nly wanted to be loved,
R espect them and they will respect you.

L onging to live long,
I f you care for them,
F un, playful and loving,
E nd all animals in their right time.

Hayley Yates (13)
Pudsey Grangefield School

Chocolate

As smooth as a baby's bottom
As different raced as humans
Sometimes brown, sometimes white
Sometimes heavy, sometimes light
But always comforting, sweet
And reassuring
I enter the middle
All with different centres
Some soft, some crunchy
Some hard, some silky
But all the same to me.

Kavita Sharma (13)
Pudsey Grangefield School

All The World's A Stage

I hear the audience file into seats,
I feel the fan blowing on me,
I smell the excitement turn into nerves,
I taste new beginnings,
As I see the actors preparing to perform,
I hear the music, played out loud,
I see the drama, to be or not to be,
I smell the tension ready to burst,
While I feel the people hustling past,
I taste my tastebuds tickle,
I hear my cue, shouted at me,
I feel hands grabbing, pulling,
I smell the air draining my lungs,
I taste my perspiration growing on my brow,
I see the audience, waiting proud.
I see the faces, expectant, waiting,
I feel their breath drawing back,
As I taste my dry mouth,
I smell my time drawing along,
And I hear my first line.

Leanne Hoang (13)
Pudsey Grangefield School

Gothic Poems

M onstrous monster,
O n a dark, stormy night,
N early creeping up to you to give you a fright,
S lowly walking down the stairs,
T here becomes a monster, scared
E ven though you're really scared,
R eally dark nights give you a fright.

Becky Thompson
Pudsey Grangefield School

Friends And Family

Friends are forever,
They'll stick by you till the end.
Whenever you're sad they're always there,
And whenever you're happy,
They're there to share the fun!

Families are just the same,
Only their love is unconditional,
Whatever happens,
Good or bad,
Your family's there to stop you feeling sad.

Friends are forever,
They'll stick by you till the end.
You'll never feel blue when they're with you,
Cos you'll know you have a friend.

Families are just the same,
Only their love is unconditional,
When all you want is the world to swallow you up,
You can rely on your family,
To make you feel loved.

So remember,
However big the crisis,
However bad the problem,
It'll be ten times better with your friends and family,
They'll stand by you through and through.

Kayleigh Higgins (13)
Pudsey Grangefield School

The Chair

Inside the cold cell I wait
To hear my fate
The walls are closing in as I take a deep breath
My sentence, *death*

Not guilty, I didn't do it
Now on the electric chair I sit
Murder, I didn't even know the guy
So I go down, just tell me why

The chair is there, I am going to die here
I'm scared, all I can feel is fear
My time is up as the clock goes ding
And I die because someone killed the king

So on the spot I lie
The security guard eating pie
In my eternal resting place
I wish I'd stayed at the base.

Joe Royce (13)
Pudsey Grangefield School

Friends

Friends are good, friends are great
I can even call them mates.
I like them, they like me
They sometimes even come for tea.

We have some fun, we have some screams
Justin Timberlake in our dreams.
My mobile goes once and then again
My mum says it will scramble my brain.

In and out, out and in
Dad wants to know where I've been.
I've been with mates to have some fun
I suppose I should get my homework done!

Vicky Huffinley (12)
Pudsey Grangefield School

Cold Night In November

I woke in the morning,
To find myself yawning,
Then I started to remember,
The cold night in November.

I curled under the bed,
Thoughts ran through my head,
I had no time to think,
Yet I nervously blink.

I got under the quilt,
My mind full of guilt,
Blocking out the sound,
Which followed me around.

I can't tell you what's wrong,
As I'm trying to be strong,
I'm trying not to remember,
The cold night in November.

Reece Fletcher (13)
Pudsey Grangefield School

She's Dead

That horrible, frightful day
When my grandma passed away
'She's dead,' I cried when my mum told me
I went to my room and that made me see
No one can live forever, not even she
I cried all day, it couldn't be true
It couldn't have happened, she wasn't dead
I didn't believe she was dead
I cried, I shouted, I even hit the wall
That couldn't make it even seem better
Her funeral would be in 2 weeks
Tears couldn't be helped
She's dead
My dear old grandma's dead.

Aidan Jones (12)
Pudsey Grangefield School

Low Below The Ocean Depths

Low below the ocean depths,
Hidden between the coral reef,
A small, mysterious creature,
Floats within the currents,
Brown and rough,
It dares not move,
Thus the ocean carries it along,
It lands upon the earth's hot surface,
Under the feet of happy siblings,
With many of its other friends,
It gets caught up in a vast container,
Wet and cold - all stuck up together,
Then they feel the ocean breeze again,
As the curtains are pulled over them,
Mother Nature calls them back,
Low below the ocean depths,
Hidden between the coral reef,
A small, mysterious creature,
Floats within the currents.
The sand.

Faisal Siddiq (13)
Pudsey Grangefield School

Netball Poem

The shooters get the ball into the net
Good players score without fret
Attackers get the ball to the shooters to score
When you have the ball keep your feet on the floor.

Centre starts off the game
None of the players are the same
The defenders defend against the other team
It gets noisy when the girls all scream
The keeper stops the other team from scoring
A game of netball is never boring.

Jodie Parker (11)
Pudsey Grangefield School

The Hidden Danger

Lurking in hidden depths,
Staying out of sight,
Slowly creeping, crawling, panting,
I run and jump, run and jump.

Weaving in and out of huge mountain boulders,
I see a treacherous and humongous sea ready to take me in,
I see my prey and launch up, up and up,
Weapons flared, wings buzzing.

I attack, instantly she reacts,
Huge and deadly limbs raking at me like claws,
I retrieve my syringe-like beak and off I go,
Wind and heat, my deadly enemies,
Wind to stop me and curb me from completing my mission,
Heat to kill me and burn my desire.

I see a magnificent abyss,
The sacred red tonic that keeps me alive,
Down I soar, faster and faster,
Picking up pace I dive, I dive.

In one quick and fluid movement,
I pierce the barrier that holds me back,
Looking around I see nothing,
Then down it comes,
Death made of plastic.

I'm gone now, far away,
Too distant to smell,
But worst of all,
Too distant to taste.

Amar Singh (14)
Pudsey Grangefield School

Stolen Speed!

The car stood unattended,
In the dark street, all alone,
The car keys hung suspended,
On her finger by the phone.

The car fired up so quickly,
With no trouble at all,
The girl started feeling sickly,
As she knew their lifespan soon could fall.

Racing down the road so fast,
Police cars at the rear,
The need for speed on an empty road,
Funeral bells they soon would hear.

A sudden slip to cause the pain,
As the car flipped over again and again,
Three lifeless bodies hung limp in the rain,
As the life of these three cannot be regained.

Charlotte Howarth (14)
Pudsey Grangefield School

The Fox

A fox came into my garden last night,
It was sharp and sly.
Its coat was silky and sleek
And it had brown, beady eyes!

It stared up into the window,
As if longing to come in.
It saw me and shot off -
As quick as a dart,
Into the dark night -
                    Hunting.

Heather Harkness (11)
Pudsey Grangefield School

My Poor Daddy

Daddy always smiles at me,
He says I'm pretty as can be.
He picks me up and twirls me round,
And carries me all the way to town.

I was young and he was old,
He wasn't tired he always told.
Until that day he dropped me so,
The reason why I just don't know.

Then one day I was at school,
The day so hot just turned so cool.
Ms Jackson told me on that day,
My poor old daddy passed away.

I'll always remember my daddy John,
We used to have fun all the day long.
And then that frightful Tuesday,
My daddy went and passed away.

I don't know why he was killed,
He wasn't even very ill,
But daddy John would always say,
'I'll love you till my dying day'.

And that day was today.

Lesley Fuzell (12)
Pudsey Grangefield School

Gothic Poem

There was once a boy called Danny
Who had a gruesome granny
He had quite a fright
In the dead of night
When his granny went barmy
Over a bleak creak
By the inhabiting ghost
But that's Danny's granny.

Thomas Dockerty (12)
Pudsey Grangefield School

Jersey

Last Saturday at ten past two
I boarded a plane
And off I flew.

To an island near France
Where I jet-skied,
Swam and danced.

The sea was blue and the sun was bright,
I went sightseeing during the day,
And went to bed late at night.

I saw a lighthouse called Corbie're,
It was surrounded by rocks,
But at low tide could I get there?

I went to the pottery and made a plate,
It had to be glazed,
So I had to wait.

The zoo was surrounded by lots of trees,
There were gorillas, monkeys,
Bears and fleas.

The underground hospital was smelly and dark,
I wish instead
I'd gone on the trip to Sark.

Jersey is a lovely place to stay,
Golden sands, rock pools,
And I hope to return one day.

Simon Pickering (12)
Pudsey Grangefield School

Computers

Technology's improving,
Every single day,
I think it is stupid,
So this is what I say,
'Go away technology,
Pen and paper rules,
Go away technology,
You are for techno fools.'
One day I used the Internet,
And all that I can say is,
The standards are not set,
I logged on very easily,
I thought it was quite measly,
But then it went all wrong,
I got onto the Internet,
It said, 'Your order has been set,
For 200 PS2s.'
I jumped, I cried,
And all I heard were woos,
Shut down the computer,
Unplugged it, smashed it too *.
The order came one Sunday night,
I put them straight out of sight,
They said for wasting all their time,
I have a small bill climb.
'Go away technology,
Pen and paper rules,
Go away technology,
You are for techno fools.'

* No computers were harmed in this poem.

Warren Hirst (12)
Pudsey Grangefield School

My Best Friend Zoe!

M y best friend is Zoe
Y ou can say she's mad

B ut just right for me
E veryone should have a best friend
S omeone you can certainly
T rust, rely on, talk to

F orever and ever, me and Zoe - best friends
R ight from the start
I knew we would be great friends
E ven though we don't go to the same school
N either of us complain
D efinitely friends till the last second of the end.

Sophie Dawson (11)
Pudsey Grangefield School

Dreams

Dream, dream of a place
a faraway place beneath starry skies or dark swamps,
where everything is true and anything is possible.
Imagine things that can't possibly be true, but they are.
And see things you wouldn't normally see.
Be transported in an instant to a place
deep within the maze of your mind
and see memories past and future.
One second be alone in a dusty desert
and next second be in a sea of faceless people
drowning in their jeers and taunts.
Then awake and not recall these remarkable images you saw.

Katie Radford (13)
Pudsey Grangefield School

A Dark Night In The Graveyard

On a dark, bleak and stormy night,
A ghost came along and gave me a fright.
I screamed, shivered and let out a screech,
I wished I was on holiday, relaxing on a beach.
But I was in the graveyard on a dark, stormy night,
When a ghost came along and gave me a fright.

I didn't know what to do, I tried to get away,
But the ghost came in front and beckoned me to stay.
For most of the night I sat and listened,
The ghost ran away as soon as the sun glistened.
But this time I didn't let out a screech,
I still wished I was on holiday, relaxing on a beach.
Even though I was in the graveyard on a dark, stormy night,
When the ghost came along and gave me a fright.

Demi Proctor (11)
Pudsey Grangefield Schoo

Gothic Poem

It was a cold, windy night in the graveyard,
All you could hear were owls hooting,
Then a loud noise was heard from the black distance.
The church window crashed open . . .
There was a big light that shone,
Why was there a light in an old abandoned church?
Who would be there?
What do they want?
Why are they there?
A girl's voice was heard,
The kids in the graveyard now got scared.
The sceptre floated towards them,
She chased . . . they ran.

Lizzie Kirby (12)
Pudsey Grangefield School

Elephant

Slow mover
Nose hoover

Floor stomper
Peanut chomper

Ear flapper
Long napper

Tusk basher
Rock smasher

Plant eater
Ground beater

Mud wallower
Water swallower

Strong and defiant
A gentle giant.

Adam Earnshaw (11)
Pudsey Grangefield School

Gothic Poems

One dark night
I had a fright
Outside the graveyard gate
Then I saw my mate
Run through the gate
Being chased by the graveyard ghoul
I saw he was such a fool
He saw the ghoul
By the graveyard light
The ghoul gave him an awful fright
Was only our Mike
My brother, dressed up for Hallowe'en night!

Lee Tunnicliffe (12)
Pudsey Grangefield School

Welcome To The Haunted House

Step in through the rusty gates -
be quiet as a mouse.
We're going to sneak and take a peek,
inside the haunted house.

An empty suit of armour
is clanking down the hall,
to a party in the ballroom -
it's the monsters' secret ball!

So while the party's in good swing,
be as quiet as a mouse.
Tiptoe out while you can -
escape the haunted house.

Joshua Woodhead (11)
Pudsey Grangefield School

My Pet Fish

As bright as a bulb,
As quiet as a mouse,
As slippery as a snake,
As golden as a coin,

Blowing bubbles every minute,
Swimming like a duck,
Eating like a lion,
As hungry as a bear.

The tank is full of water,
That is where it lives,
He is there day and night,
Swimming with delight.

Leon Chang (11)
Pudsey Grangefield School

There Was A Girl

There was a girl
Who stood alone,
She's been like this
As long as she'd known,

People refused to talk to her,

In the skies
Like every other day,
Chilled,
Black and grey,

Came a light,
Bright,
And,
White,

Took her to a place
Unknown,
The middle of nowhere,
Not like home,

She looked all around,
Down,
Left and right,

Then she looked up,
Glaring at the sun,
Then joyfully,
Started to run,

Her wish had come true,
There was warmth, brightness too,

Some said she wished too soon,
Some said she wished too long,
Till one winter day,
She was gone!

Emma Jane Teasdale (12)
Pudsey Grangefield School

War

War is cruel,
Unkind and evil,
Painful and bloody,
Souls are lost and hearts are broken.

Men fighting and guns firing,
Planes bombing, men running,
Ships shooting and tanks crushing,
Towns on fire, deserted and lifeless.

Men of power, hungry and greedy,
Lives lost for meaningless reasons,
Women crying and children dying,
Is this cinema and TV games
Or has reality been lost
In the search for entertainment?

Nathan Gasser (11)
Pudsey Grangefield School

Football Crazy

F ootball is life
O f course it is to me
O bviously others don't agree
T eams I play for
B alls I have played with
A ll the teams we've beaten and lost have been great
L eagues and friendly games I've played
L ots of fun I've had too.

Tommy Payne (11)
Pudsey Grangefield School

My Cat

I have a cat which is my pet
He hates to visit our nearby vet
Once he fell and hurt his foot
His wrist was bruised, his back was cut.

He came to the door, cold and wet
He had no choice but to visit the vet
He got a plaster put on his paw
His back still cut and very sore.

Now he's home,quiet and fed
Lying by the window in his bed
He's sat waiting, wanting to go out
Soon he'll be up and wandering about.

Rebecca Wilkinson (11)
Pudsey Grangefield School

Pyramids

Pyramids - nobody can move them
As big as a dinosaur
As large as a house
A container of dead people
A valuable storer
A golden palace
An upside-down ice cream cone
A pointed dagger
A sharp stinger
Pyramids -
A monumental structure.

Matthew Nicholson (12)
Pudsey Grangefield School

My Friends

My friends are Georgie, Danni and Sam
Another is called Sophie
Who hangs in our gang.
We are hippy, chic and cool.
We always hang together when we're at school
Georgie is great, short and fun
Sam's hair is golden like the sun
Danni is tall and always brings food
Sophie is calm and hardly ever in a mood
Another's called Ella who is really smart
When we're together our friendship won't part.
We never leave anyone out
We try to smile not groan or pout.

Friendship is good for me and you.
Friendship is good for animals too.

Claire Aithne Dring (11)
Pudsey Grangefield School

Autumn

As the wind blew gracefully and oh so elegantly
through the tall trees.
Overflowing with crusty leaves in a spectrum of colours,
waiting to be blown to a new home.
The sunbeams reflect an angry amber colour.
Strolling past, observing the view of my shadow
dancing on the energetic flames, oh so satisfying.
Whistle, whistle, howl, howl, the autumn winds sound.
Me, the wind and life, all oh so identical, all unique.
The trees, the sun, the wind will always be a reminder of me,
life and autumn.

Emily Lynn (11)
Pudsey Grangefield School

At Home

When you are at home you feel safe and secure.
You don't worry about being scared or hurt.
People at home are people you know and you are sure.
That times will be good and life will be great!

When you are at home the family is there.
To help you when you are stuck or in need.
Your family will be there when you cannot bear;
The trouble and frustration of your life.

When you are at home the life you live is good.
You have the shelter to stop the weather from hurting you.
Homes are the safest places on Earth.
They are the best places to be.

When you are at home you feel safe and secure.

Joseph Scaife (11)
Pudsey Grangefield School

War

War starts but never seems to end,
It breaks the world apart.
Why can't we ever leave to mend?
Never letting a war start.

Stop all the killing and the shooting,
Stop all the poor from looting.
Anger should be calm and flowing,
Like a stream that starts growing.

People should be kind to each other,
We should love and care for one another.

Jessica Wilkinson (11)
Pudsey Grangefield School

Pick On Someone Else

Bullies are mean,
they are so keen,
to act so tough,
they play so rough.
They spoil our games
and call us names,
they hit and shout
and mess about.
They make us cry
and don't tell us why,
we do not know,
why they do it so.
We should maybe fight back,
punch, kick and slap,
but then we're as bad
as the bullies, and they're *sad!*

Joshua-Lee Warriner (11)
Pudsey Grangefield School

Hobbies

H aving fun in the park with my friends.
O ne-nil final score and the joy of winning at last.
B oxing match again tonight - punching (throwing a jab and hook).
B eginning my game on the PS2, FIFA my favourite for now!
I n the house - wrestling with Luke, this time I'm going to win.
E xcellent bike ride. I win and my heart beats like a drum.
S imple day, over and done, hobbies are number one.

Finlay Pattison (11)
Pudsey Grangefield School

In The Park

In the park
It's not so dark
When the moon is full
But when it's full
The air is cold and grim.

I went to the park
To spy a lark
At the break of day
So there I lay
In the park to spy a lark.

While I waited
Something happened
Far beyond a dream
I heard a noise
From on the hill
It was the monster
Making his evening kill.

I was so still and the trees
Were full of movement
So I saw my lark in the park
When the moon was full.

Rebecca Stephenson (12)
Pudsey Grangefield School

The Snow

S now is like a sheet of wool laying on the ground.
N ot icy but soft and fluffy.
O n the roof and on the ground.
W indow ledges as well!

Philippa Brown (11)
Pudsey Grangefield School

Christmas

Outside the street glows,
With all the promises of the season.

Decorations hang from tree to tree,
Twisting and turning like a snake.

A big white blanket on the floor,
With twinkling lights making it glimmer.

Happiness and eagerness filling little children,
Getting the magic feeling that Christmas is coming.

Trees very heavy with great mounds of white weight,
Shining and sparkling under the streetlight.

Cold, frosty air wrapping around people,
Whilst they are walking, leaving footprints behind.

People holding on for dear life,
Trying not to slip on the icy ground.

At last the children are asleep,
Whilst the presents are waiting to be unwrapped.

Tania Hussain (12)
Pudsey Grangefield School

My Cats

My cats give me pleasure,
when they sleep.
My cats give me joy,
when I stroke them.
Cats are cuddlesome,
cats are playful,
they're my friends forever.

Samantha Kitson (11)
Pudsey Grangefield School

Frankenstein

As soon as I laid eyes on him
I felt really weak and thin
He was a strange, ugly-looking man
He made me go white and lose my tan
It was the Frankenstein!
It was a scary place in time
Its hand turned into a powerful fist
I saw it shoot at me through the eerie mist
Its clothes were torn, ragged and slightly too small
I tripped and felt myself fall
I ran and felt the branches against my face
It followed and gave up chase
It was Frankenstein!
Thank God my life was still mine.

Daniel Thackery (12)
Pudsey Grangefield School

Feelings

F ury, when my brother and sister refuse to leave me alone,
E xcited, when I go with my family away from our home.
E mptiness, when I feel lonely and there is nobody there,
L oved, when I'm hugged; I know my mum and dad care.
I nsecure, when I'm at school my friends leave me out
N auseous, when I'm too long in the car my head spins about,
G lad, when the weekend's here, and we get to have fun,
S cared, of the feelings hidden inside - how do I escape them,
    Where do I run?

Laura Nicholas-Riley (11)
Pudsey Grangefield School

Poaching

Yesterday it ran across the plains,
Jumped, played and was alive.
Now he lies blooded on the ground,
A poor creature, helpless, motionless.
Yesterday it was a free soul,
Free to do what it pleased,
But now his life has been savagely ripped from his clutches.
The brutal, barbaric monster that did this just for fun,
Just for a laugh and to entertain itself,
Doesn't care.
Doesn't care that it has wasted an innocent life.
A pure life.
This man is better known as a *murderer* and a *poacher*.

Charlotte Rafton (12)
Pudsey Grangefield School

Dolphins

Dolphins swim extremely fast,
Through the misty waters,
Over the choppy waves they go,
Skimming the waves with their stomach.

Leaping gracefully out of the water,
Here, there and everywhere,
Not making a splash or a single sound,
As graceful as the sunset.

Dolphins are as friendly as a man's best friend,
They are so intelligent,
They swim so elegantly in front of me,
Like beautiful white horses in the sea.

Charlie Roberts (12)
Pudsey Grangefield School

Television Set

Dear Roald Dahl, how dare you disgrace,
The wonderful TV set sitting in its place.
You've really hurt it, it feels so sad,
Those awful words you said, so bad.
How on earth could people not like,
Such a fantastic thing for your delight.
Than reading a book about long ago lands,
I'd rather eat my own left hand.
Such excitement and fun the television set brings,
Kids channels, news channels, all sorts of things.
Kids from all over the world would flee,
To anywhere so they could watch TV.

It's a worldwide phenomena, everyone agrees,
Televisions you can hear, televisions you can see.
All the benefits the TV can give,
It would suit all people and the way they live.
Teletext, recording, twin tuners too.
Over 700 channels for me and you.
If you look in every home,
Trust me you won't be alone.
Because everyone has one, as you can see,
The fantastic invention, of course, it's the TV.
How boring and sad reading would be,
If you sat all day and didn't watch TV.
So if you don't have a television set,
Prepare to be very upset.
The television is a fantastic creation,
Nobody should even think to hate 'em
Absolutely nobody should hate 'em.
Books, throw 'em out, they're so old,
Now get a television installed!

Luke Battensby (12)
Pudsey Grangefield School

Colours Turn To Grey!

A father sits with his head in his hands,
He sees a world full of pain.
Can he imagine how the future will be,
When colours turn to grey?

A mother is rocking her baby to sleep,
She does not want her to wake.
The mother's crying out, 'Oh help me God.'
When colours turn to grey.

Noises I hear all around the town,
Fire destroys my home,
Bombs are scattered all around the town,
When colours turn to grey.

Newspaper pictures that stare from the page
Tell all the world filled with pain,
Can we imagine how the future will be
When colours turn to grey?

Laura Atkins (11)
Pudsey Grangefield School

The Try Scorer

Tall as a door,
Black as mud,
Muscles as firm as steel,
Sweaty as if he'd been out in the rain,
Hot as an oven,
Glad, as if they had won the match.

Jordan Irving (11)
Pudsey Grangefield School

Homeless

Do I annoy you?
These days I struggle through
You blank me in the street
Off to your friends you greet.

Each night is so cold
This old plastic cup I hold.
Could you spare some change?
They laugh at me, I fill with rage.

Who am I?
Don't you know?
I am the one on the bridge.
The one you walk past.
The one you laugh at.
The one who asks you for change.
Perhaps a Big Issue Madam?
Will it kill you?

Joe Hunter   (13)
Pudsey Grangefield School

My Pets

My pets are very strange,
And I have a very wide range
Of cats and dogs and bees and frogs
All of which I like.

7 cats and 13 dogs
And a whopping number of 22 frogs
Mice that squeak
And parrots that squawk
Sometimes I swear I hear them talk.

A cat called Ginger
And a dog called Scruff.
But if I told you much more
I'm sure you'd have heard enough.

Rebecca Matthews   (12)
Pudsey Grangefield School

October

Summer seems far away
As we walk through the park on a cold afternoon
Autumn is here, leaves falling
Colours changing . . . it will be winter soon.

Leaves chase each other, round and round
Branches move to and fro
The noise of the wind through the trees
Swishing, swaying, blowing.

Squirrels searching for food
Chestnuts and acorns cover the ground
Rustling through the leaves
Shush! Don't make a sound.

Dogs chase each other, rough and tumble
Following seagulls as they fly
People in big coats and hats
Watching the clouds dance in the sky.

Head for home, cold and tired
Wind settling as we walk towards the house
Kettle on, warm cup of tea
Sit down, relax, everything quiet as a mouse!

Olivia Hawksworth (12)
Pudsey Grangefield School

The Vampire Of Sunderland

In the graveyard buried deep
Lays the most feared vampire of Sunderland.

He sneers through the dark mist
And makes the sound of an angry snake hiss
As he gives the cold kiss.

Luke Hird (13)
Pudsey Grangefield School

The Ocean

The ocean is a blanket,
Covering the land.
Lapping up and spraying you,
Tickling the sand.

We dream of being by the sea,
Paddling and having fun.
Running round on the beach,
Have an ice cream, but which one?

The ocean is a home,
For creatures such as fish.
I'd love to be at the shore,
Clear water is my wish.

Kate Heathcote (12)
Pudsey Grangefield School

Think

Think of all the suffering in this world
Think about all the homeless people
With no food on their plates
Or a bed to sleep on.

Think of children crying
As their houses are bombed
With nor mothers or fathers
To comfort them.

Just take a moment
To think about people with no homes
Or children with no parents
Just think of all the cruelty in the world.

Sam Harton (12)
Pudsey Grangefield School

My Family

I have a very little family,
I mean by the size
And just because we're brainy
Doesn't mean we're wise.

I love my family very much,
I know it's hard to say.
But I don't try to show it,
There is never a way.

I always try to find a way,
I really, really do.
I really think they love me,
But not really true.

I'll try and finish off
By saying these few words.
'My family is the best,
Better than the rest.'

Thomas McHale (11)
Pudsey Grangefield School

My Dog

I have a dog called Bruno
He likes to bark and wag his tail
I like to call him Uno
He jumps up at me and makes me feel quite frail.

His fur is soft, black and white
When he goes out he looks like the night
He has another dog friend called Mack
When I throw a tennis ball he brings it back.

John Larner (11)
Pudsey Grangefield School

The Poetry Competition

Who will win the competition?
Will it be me or my friend?
It might be someone from my school
Or somebody totally different.

I wonder who the judges are
Or if it's done by a computer system?
If only I knew what the future held
If only I could tell.

The only thing I know
Is it will be someone from Leeds
Whether it will be a boy or girl
Or maybe a teenager.

No one knows what will happen
One day to the next
All we know is what we know
Not what's in the future.

Jade Fretwell (11)
Pudsey Grangefield School

Shopping

S hopping is what I do best
H owever my bedroom's a mess
O n top of my wardrobe is all my stuff
P utting them there whilst I was in a big huff
P lacing everything in the bin
 I t seems such a sin
N eeding, needing lots of tops
G oing shopping doesn't half rock!

Jeni Casey (13)
Pudsey Grangefield School

Summertime

Now that summertime has come
The sun shining bright every day
And the laughter of children having fun

Now it's time to put on your summer wear
So now enjoy the lovely weather
For summertime is here at last

The flowers in full bloom
Dance happily in the breeze
Lots of daisies waiting to be chained

Wander through the lush green meadows
Beautiful flowers waiting to be picked
Fragrance of lavender fills the air

So make the most of summertime
As soon it will fade away
But wonder not as it will be back someday.

Claire Davies (11)
Pudsey Grangefield School

Winter Days

Winter's day with frosty fingers.
Ice-cold windowpane.
Snowman in the garden.
Snow fights down the lane.
Frosted trees with covered snow.
Icy winter's winds
Makes the children laugh and play,
While little robin sings.

Oliver Howes (12)
Pudsey Grangefield School

Poor Little Spider

Poor little spider,
Sat in the corner,
Feeling sorry for himself.

His legs are slender, spiky and strong
And he lives on his web by the shelf.

Poor little spider,
Sat in the corner,
Spinning a web like gold.

His body is round like a conker in its shell
And he makes people's blood run cold.

Poor little spider,
Sat in the corner,
Looking for some flies to eat.

His eyes are shiny pinheads
And he has suckers stuck to his feet.

Poor little spider,
Sat in the corner,
With a heart that's full of fear.

Poor little spider,
Sat in the corner,
People are getting near . . . s*plat!*

Sophie Hudson (12)
Pudsey Grangefield School

Family

F is for families are helpful and happy
A is for aunties, uncles and cousins
M is for mums, dads and brothers
 I is for it's sometimes not funny but they're still always there
L is for loving you all the time
Y is for you and your family that's all you need.
   So be happy with your family.

India Haresign (11)
Pudsey Grangefield School

Horrid Homework

I pull out my exercise book
laughing with all of my mates,
when I suddenly realise the date.
Oh no! Homework was meant to be in today.
I hear those dreaded words, 'Homework out class!'
My hands go sweaty, sweat drips off them as clear as glass.
I try and think of a good excuse
But he's heard it all before like . . .

On Monday I was out at town.
On Tuesday I was feeling down.
On Wednesday my dog ate it.
On Thursday I was squeezing my mate's big zits!
On Friday I was out buying the Black Eyed Peas' song.
On Saturday I was swimming the seas.

'Vanessa Greenhalgh! Why haven't you done your homework?'
'Sorry Sir, but my . . . nana went berserk!'
'And on Sunday? You haven't said anything about Sunday.'
'Well, I was making my energy preserve.'

Vanessa Greenhalgh (11)
Pudsey Grangefield School

Family, Friends And Feelings

Feeling happy
Feeling sad
Feeling really, really bad.

My family is there to love and care.
With a problem I can always share.

My friends are good
And sometimes bad
But when I'm with them I'm never sad.

Whether I'm with my friends or family
I'm always feeling very happy.

Matthew Popple (11)
Pudsey Grangefield School

Chester

He is brown and white and oh so cute,
He keeps warm in his fluffy suit,
His ears are floppy and he is sometimes sloppy,
His eyes are shiny, oh so bright,
They twinkle like the stars at night,
He jumps up and down, he's always in a scurry,
And when he eats his tasty treat he does it in a hurry,
He does not sleep in a bed, he sleeps on lots of hay,
And makes me very happy when I see him every day,
When Chester is asleep he dreams of running free,
But he is very happy when he cuddles up to me,
I didn't want a kitten and I didn't want a parrot,
He's my bunny and he loves me like his carrot.

Connor Smith (11)
Pudsey Grangefield School

Forever Friends

When I left school I was feeling down
But then I met some friends, which turned around my frown
There's Rheane, India, Laura, Jade and Amy
And guess what? I'm the baby!
We have a good laugh together
I'm sure we'll be good friends forever
I still miss my old friends
But my new friends are loopy and round the bend
We are special in one way or another
I may be the baby but I act like their mother
I'm alright now, I have a smile on my face
And my new friends are, well, ace!

Stephanie Day (11)
Pudsey Grangefield School

Bullies

Bullies are mean
Bullies are so keen,
They pack a punch
In every lunch.

Bullies are a menace
So they will like tennis,
They are rough stuff
To think they're tough.

For your attention
I would like to mention,
For the prevention
Here is your suspension.

Jack Goult (11)
Pudsey Grangefield School

My Niece Kaye

My niece is called Kaye
You should hear what she can say
She is an active child
Or shall I say wild
She is funny and cute
She would look smart in a suit
She's like a cuddly bear
That we would never want to tear
She's only one
And loves to have fun
She was born three months before May
That's my niece Kaye.

Katrina Hoang (13)
Pudsey Grangefield School

Teddies, Teddies Everywhere

Teddies, teddies, everywhere.
'But where's my teddy? Where oh where?
I've lost my teddy, oh no!'
Well it's not under my pillow
It's not under my blankey
I need a hanky
And it's not under my bed!
I feel like I'm going to loose my head
Oh where oh where can my teddy be,
I remember now, I left him downstairs
While having my tea!

Jade Pinnion (11)
Pudsey Grangefield School

Elephant

Elephants are very happy,
They are as large as Earth,
Elephants are as intelligent as the brainiest man on Earth,
Elephants are so heavy that an earthquake can occur,
When they walk by the buildings shake
And everyone shouts 'Earthquake!'
They have big feet so I would watch out,
They have inquisitive trunks.

Helen Rothery (12)
Pudsey Grangefield School

The Sun And Moon

The colossal moon perches, clinging in the night mist,
The sun sits on the contrasting verge of the cosmos
And the sun doesn't give the light to the moon
Assuming the moon's gonna owe him one,
And they both stare down at the huge blue and green marble
Below them and they chuckle to each other!

Adam Trotter (13)
Pudsey Grangefield School

Roxy

My dog's name is Roxy;
because she looks a bit foxy!
She loves to go for walks;
and sometimes I'm sure she tries to talk!
She's always pleased to see me
especially when it's time for tea!
She usually does as she's told;
and really is as good as gold!

Thomas Greenwood (11)
Pudsey Grangefield School

The Spider Poem

Wall crawler,
Parachute faller,
Plughole lurker,
Many-eyed smirker,
Web spinner,
The fly's a dinner.

Lewis Wray (11)
Pudsey Grangefield School

Friends

F riends are forever
R emember to stick together
I n groups and gangs
E veryone shares things
N o one lies
D on't forget to stick together
S hare secrets.

Laura Beel (12)
Pudsey Grangefield School

The Four Seasons - Haikus

Red beautiful plants
New spring crops in farmers' fields
Spring chill fills the air.

Colourful flowers
Growing brightly in the park
Smelling beautiful.

Very crispy leaves
Shining brown conkers falling
Golden skies dying.

Very snowy hills
Christmas just round the corner
Ice on window sills.

Daniel Davis (11)
Rodillian School

Spider On The Bed

Crawling over the huge desert,
A quilt thrown over a king-sized bed,
A stripe of blue like a river,
Blocking the way to freedom,
Cushions like a never-ending mountain,
Looming over me,
The posts of the bed
Like towers in the distance,
Cuddly teddies squeezed into corners,
Like an army of giants chasing me,
I ran and ran with my eight long legs.

Clayton Stott (11)
Rodillian School

Me At School

I dash around the school
Trying to get to class,
Then suddenly I get
Knocked off my feet by a giant.
I crawl to the side
And quickly got up
Trying to look cool
But before I can creep away
An even bigger giant
Grabs hold of me
And pulls me towards him,
'Why are you on the floor?'
'P-p-p-please sir,'
I stutter,
'I just got knocked over!'

Sophie France (12)
Rodillian School

Sparky And Sky

Sparky and Sky are my pets
Sky my rabbit jumps and hops
Plays and scampers
Until he flops.

Sparky my dog
Scampers and slides
Dashes and darts
He runs, jumps and he leaps
And falls asleep.

Reece Bryan (12)
Rodillian School

The World In White

A soft white blanket,
Crystals falling from the cold, white sky,
Snowmen in the snow,
Standing with chilly toes,
Winter is here.

Silence as cold air rushes by,
A lonely glove with running dye,
Crispy brown leaves blowing by,
Winter is here.

Frosted windows, silver webs,
White painted roofs on cars and sheds,
Red ears and white bobble hats,
Blue noses and shivering cats,
Winter is here.

Lit up fires and windows shut,
Keyholes covered and firewood cut,
Plants all dead,
Lonely parks,
There's only one thing that this all marks,
Winter is here.

Lesley Sharp (12)
Rodillian School

Ant

How magnified things must appear,
to a tiny ant in a huge room.

Dusters like sky-high trees,
tissues like blankets on a bed,
pans like reflective mirrors,
mugs like volcanoes, full with liquid,
plates like smooth, icy lakes,
bottles like empty locked rooms.

Elizabeth Hartley (11)
Rodillian School

An Insect Poem

How large must I seem
to a tiny bumblebee
A pencil case is like a mountain;
a tin of beans like a swimming pool.

A light bulb like a blazing fire,
my bracelet is an electric wire.
A pencil is like the Eiffel Tower
compared to these, a bee has little power.

A bag of crisps is a mighty feast,
to a bee, I am a beast.
So, next time you think, 'I am little me!'
Just think of this small, harmless bee.

Rhian Holland (11)
Rodillian School

The Fly

Humans are like giants against me,
The fish in the lake which is like an open sea to me,
They catch goldfish
They're the golden whales to me,
As I fly past ants
It's just like a traffic jam,
When I fly, I have to watch out
For a horrible thing . . . *spiders!*
They're like black demons of doom,
Their web is like a huge fishing net
It's just a big world out there!

Sophie Thomas (11)
Rodillian School

The Flea

Could you imagine to be a little flea,
Jumping around on four little legs
And as tiny as could be?

A football as big as a mountain
And a wardrobe like the world,
A book just like a domino
That falls over curled!

A footstep like an earthquake
And a word like a brass band,
A feather like a ton of bricks,
That feels like an elastic band.

A car as big as an elephant
And a bath just like the sea,
A tap just like a waterfall,
That could even drown me!

A snowball like a cannonball,
And a snowflake like a pea,
A droplet like a rainfall
That wouldn't harm me.

Rachel Whitlam (11)
Rodillian School

A Supermarket

Trolleys and babies,
Apples and bananas,
Jelly, ice cream
Eating and drinking
Sausages, bacon, crisps and beans
Pens and pencils
Apple pie and custard
Bread and butter.

Laura Barker (11)
Rodillian School

Her

Her lips like juicy cherries.
Her cheeks like the reddest rose.
Her eyes like the deep blue sea.
Her hair like ebony.

Her smile like the dawn of a day.
Her laughter like the soft breeze.
Her tears like the gentle rain.
Her singing like the kind birds in the morning.

Her kisses like a light touch of a feather.
Her hugs like a big bear.
Her mind like a calculator.
Her sadness like a black cloud.

Emma Scothorn (11)
Rodillian School

At Home

Television talking
Birds are squawking
Mum's washing up
Dad is putting down his cup
Kettle boiling
Washer toiling
Computer keyboard clicking
Clock ticking
Fire roaring
Grandad's snoring.

Billy Harris (11)
Rodillian School

Me And My Team

Passing and swerving
Dodging and turning,
Kicking and running.
Pushing out of the way
Slipping and sliding
On the mud.
People fighting
As they would.
Fans are screaming,
We're still playing
Our heart and souls out.
It's coming to the end.
We dance
After winning the cup.

Stuart Biscomb (11)
Rodillian School

Ravenous Dog

A head like a cone,
A nose like spilt black ink,
A mouth like a shark's,
An ear like a spike,
A neck as short as a pencil stub,
Legs as thick as a tree trunk,
A body the weight of a tonne.

Matthew Lund (11)
Rodillian School

Seasons

Spring
White daisies blooming,
White fluffy lambs waking up,
White frost disappears.

Summer
The bright yellow sun,
Wakes us up in the morning
And glows like real gold.

Autumn
The green, crispy leaves
And the windy, dark mornings,
The cold rainy days.

Winter
The pure, wet, white snow
And the tall, fat round snowmen
The gifts at Christmas.

Emma Andrews (11)
Rodillian School

A Rabbit

Head like a nut inside its shell,
A nose like a cherry,
Mouth like a rat's tail,
An ear like a leaf,
Neck like a stump,
A body like an upside-down bowl
And leopard's legs.

Georgia-Blue Rayson (11)
Rodillian School

The Ant

How long until the ant sees small things?
When the ant walks in the garden it sees,
Tall pieces of grass like a never-ending forest.

How long until the ant sees small things?
When the ant walks in the garden it sees,
Large plant pots like large government buildings.

How long until the ant sees small things?
When the ant walks in the garden it sees,
A large garden shed like the king's grand palace.

How long until the ant sees small things?
When the ant walks in the garden it sees,
A garden wall like a barrier of defence.

How long until the ant sees small things?
When the ant walks in the garden it sees,
At last an insect the same as him,
Now he can go home in peace.

Thomas Hart (12)
Rodillian School

The Beach

Squawking seagulls, silky sand,
Creamy ice cream, juice in the sand.
Children playing, fish in buckets,
People eating fish and chips.
Adults roasting, melting kids,
Ponies, donkeys, boats and ships.
People surfing, dolphins swimming,
Look at everyone, they're all . . .
Smiling!

Victoria Winn (11)
Rodillian School

Me And My Team

As I dodge and weave
with my team
sprint and tackle
me and my team
slide over, try
for me and my team
slip and slide, twist and turn
for me and my team
encouraging words shout in as a team
weave and turn
through and defence
me and my team
we've won the match
me and my team.

Robert Turpin (11)
Rodillian School

Outside

Cars whishing, trees rushing
Windows slamming, cars crashing
Cows mooing, tractors flowing
Flowers dying, water pouring
Building banging, birds singing
Grass growing, people talking
Mobiles ringing, people running
Wind whistling, ball banging.

Samantha Abbey (11)
Rodillian School

Sound Effect Poem

Smash! goes the sizzling sea
Crash! goes the cracked cans as they hit the floor.
As the paper rustles,
As the pop popped,
As the sausages sizzled away,
As the people pushed in the crowds
At a football match.
Dogs are dirty as a puddle of mud,
Cats as cute as a newborn baby,
Fish are all kinds of tropical colours,
But best of all a horse
With beautiful, long, glittery, shiny, silver hair.

Nathaniel Lunn (11)
Rodillian School

Tortoise

It has a head shaped like a balloon,
A body shaped like a giant plate,
Legs like a frog,
A nose like a small ball,
A mouth shaped just like a goldfish,
A neck as long as a giraffe
And an ear like an octopus,
But as slow as a snail.

Kimberley McDonnell (11)
Rodillian School

The Lion

Eyes like a tennis ball
As bright as the moon, pearly-white
Teeth like knives
As sharp as scissors

Claws like a disaster
Waiting to happen
Hair like a ball of string
Also as spiky as a cactus

A roar like a stereo
As loud as a storm
A tail like a spring
As bouncy as Tigger.

Natalie Kelly (11)
Rodillian School

Dogs

A body like a pumped up bean bag,
Legs like a thick twig,
A neck like a human,
An ear like a bear,
A mouth like a cat,
A nose like a pig,
A head like a rounded rugby ball,
A tail like a stone.

Melissa Wilson (11)
Rodillian School

The Caterpillar

I'm climbing the plant
getting higher and higher
finding it hard to keep holding on.
I'm light as a feather
but the leaves keep swaying me
from side to side.

It feels like I'm going on forever
like going up a mountain top
will I ever get to the top
without falling off?

Is this a plant or is it a tree?
It's taken me hours
to get this far,
but one of these days
I will make it.

Keeley Westerman (11)
Rodillian School

Listen

Clicking of pens
Rustling of paper
Computers buzzing
Squeaking of chairs
Shuffling of feet
Shouting of children
Banging of feet
Banging rulers
Whistling
Children coughing
Noise around me.

Sonya Taylor (11)
Rodillian School

Sports Kit

Red and white,
Blue and green,
Footballers on the telly screen,
Leeds are winning one-nil,
People pay their ticket bill,
Whistles, flags,
Hats and bags,
All flying in the crowd.

Dale Gregory (11)
Rodillian School

The Beach

Buckets and spades
Ice cream vans
Boys and girls
Mums and dads.

Lollies and ice cream
Fish and chips
Donkeys and beachballs
Bright and beautiful.

Jessica Hartley (11)
Rodillian School

The Big-Footed Rhinoceros

Got horns bigger than elephant tusks,
They clean themselves in the space where fish go,
As dirty as mud can be,
Practically as noisy as a dinosaur needing help,
Has got bigger feet than ten koi carp put together.

Hannah Eatwell (12)
Rodillian School

My Dog

Dashing 'n' darting
Round the house
Slipping 'n' sliding
Chasing a mouse
Skid, skid
Fell over
Into a kid
Across the floor
Round Mum
Down the stairs
Oh, what a nightmare!

Rhiannon Latham (11)
Rodillian School

Boo!

Big and small,
run and jog,
crawl and creep,
stop and stay,
swim and dive,
walk towards you,
silent under the bed,
the cupboards are creaking,
a slightest tap on the floor,
'It's a ghost!'

Joseph Russell (11)
Rodillian School

Supermarket

Tasty burgers, chips,
Creamy ice cream,
Juicy oranges, pips
And the tomato team.

Healthy lettuce,
Wobbly jelly,
Liquorice lace
And a huge telly.

Yum, yum sweets
And fizzy Coke,
There'll be many treats,
Uh oh, my mum's broke.

Emily Webster (11)
Rodillian School

My Garden

As I walk out into my garden
I can feel the breeze come past me,
Like a large working fan in my face.
The grass swaying side to side,
Like when my hair flicks.
I hold tighter to my coat as it gets windier
My windows are banging
Birds start to find new nests
Nature is the word
For this calm day.

Demi Rickerby (11)
Rodillian School

Vampire

An ill-fitting cloak,
His piercing eyes,
His mortal charms,
A slaughter,
A nocturnal creature.

Gets pleasure from blood,
Shrieks when he's near,
Relief when he's far,
Blood lover,
Sunshine hater.

Matthew Gill (12)
St Thomas Á Becket RC School, Wakefield

Life And Love

Life is a darkness
And wenth light thou see,
Love thou shalt have
But thou art blind,
For thou art in the Devil's snare
And pain shalt embrace thou,
But thou shalt step,
Once again into Satan's snare,
Because of hope and . . . lust.

Joseph Clarke (13)
St Thomas Á Becket RC School, Wakefield

Anger

I glared and stared at her,
I ignored her as much as I could,
I tripped and kicked,
I stood on her bag,
How dare she go off
With the new girl.
She tried to talk,
I just ignored her,
Remembering the firewall of fury,
I could not let cool down
And quickly burned up inside.
But then I felt the loneliness deep within me.
The fire died down.
Gone was the frown
And as I called my friend,
I felt the last flame
Flicker out inside me.

Louise Boardall (13)
The Brooksbank School

Santa Claus

A red-wearer
A pie-eater
A present-giver
A festive-bringer
A chimney-traveller
A bell-jingler
A reindeer-stroker
A sleigh-rider
A sherry-drinker.

James Noble (12)
The Brooksbank School

The City, The Sky

A cloud forms over a bustling city,
Like a great grey bird blocking out the sun,
More of these clouds as big as twelve elephants form,
Splat! the first drop of rain falls on the city,
More and more rain comes.

The town as wet as a river,
The people pushing purposely to get away,
The sun no longer in its place,
Thunder roaring like a lion,
This liquid misery falls on the city.

No longer is the blue sky visible,
Nothing left to see,
Lightning strikes a flash like a torch,
One bustling city,
Now a shallow river.

Luke Bartey (11)
The Brooksbank School

Riddle Of The Water

I gazed down into the crystal clear water,
Winding and weaving along its course.
Splish splashing over stones,
Rushing here and rushing there.
With no time to stop and no time to spare,
Flowing freely, nothing could get in its way.
At times gliding along its chosen route,
At others its mood angry and impatient.
Tossing obstacles from its path,
Leaves and branches feeling its wrath.
Where did it come from?
Where was it going?
What was it saying?
Would I ever find out?
Please tell me what the river's all about!

Grace Alsancak (11)
The Brooksbank School

Teacher

As I sit at my desk at the front of the room,
Feeling depressed all doom and gloom,
As my pupils file in to make up a class,
Fidgeting around, not settling down fast.

I try to do the register but they won't quieten down,
I screw up my eyebrows, increasing my everlasting frown,
My chair squeaks as I stand to confront the class,
Whose aim in life is for me to harass.

'Stop that Lucy, put that down Ben,
David will you please give up chewing on that pen,
Felicity stop talking and put your gum in the bin,
Michael, stop flicking that ruler and stop whistling Lynn!'

Five minutes to go and I'm feeling unwell,
My favourite thing ever is hearing that bell,
At half-past three I hear it wail,
Now I can finally escape from this jail!

Helena Gaukroger (13)
The Brooksbank School

Football

Running down the pitch,
100 miles per hour,
Shirt's starting to itch,
It's the speed of human power.

Golden boots shoot,
It's a glorious goal,
All of the crowd hoots,
The goalie smacked into the pole.

The whistle sounds,
Shirts are swapped,
Fans leave the grounds
Corks are popped.

Kelsey Cheesbrough (11)
The Brooksbank School

Divorce

At first I didn't know, I didn't understand,
The second time I knew, it felt like it had been planned.

As I became older my dad slipped away,
I feel like a forgotten daughter every single day.
With a family of his own I don't matter anymore,
The no-loving disease is eating away at the core.

After years of pain a bigger and better dad,
Eventually a smile upon my face that once I never had.
His family took in mine and gave us a new life,
But the second time it struck like a knife.

After bringing me up for 7 years
And drying out all of my tears
I'm now forever stuck in the middle,
Everything seems to be a complicated riddle.

Living in 2 houses not one to call a home,
Life is a suitcase, feeling all alone.

Laura Crossley (13)
The Brooksbank School

The Grim Reaper

A death bringer
A pain giver
A soul taker
A sorrow maker
A heart breaker
A flesh slicer
A blood shedder
A bone breaker
A crow caller
A cloak wearer
A black rider.

Philip Nelson (12)
The Brooksbank School

Stalker

The wind blew
the trees rustled
but I trailed on
the clouds up in the dark sky

Resembled that of pirate ships
sailing along the calm black sky.
I was alone
at least that's what I thought.

I had got lost in the dark, misty forest.
then I heard footsteps.
I froze,
the blood drained from my body.

Then all of a sudden
silence entered the forest.
The moonlight projected a light picture
like a silhouette through the cave of trees.

Which looked like the figure
of a man as it crept towards me.
I ran, tripped over a rock,
then blackness . . .

Ashley Agnew (11)
The Brooksbank School

The Splinter

It's there all the time,
Like an irritating habit,
Stuck deeply in my mind,
A splinter to my brain.
I try to escape
This never-ending circle.
It's like running on a treadmill
Or a baby's emerging scream.
The endless journeys,
The used-up petrol,
Lots of new faces
But still no explanations.
Not making school,
Not knowing what's next,
Being behind in lessons
And missing on all the fun,
A splinter in my brain.
A throb up in my head.
It's a migraine,
The dreadful, horrible migraine.

Rebecca Wright (13)
The Brooksbank School

My Poem

Some of the things I like
Are rough, raging rugby
Because you smash them down.

The exotic smell of cocktails
Because the fruity flavour
Slithers down your throat.

But what I like most of all is
Snuggly cuddles with my friends and my mum
Because they make me feel warm and happy.

Some of the things I hate are small, scary spiders
Because they creep around the house waiting for you.

The stinking smell of sewage works
Because the smell lurks around.

But what I hate most of all is
Meddling-with-your-mind maths
Because it is boring, complicated and tiresome.

Beth Dawson (12)
The Brooksbank School

My First True Love

I will never forgive my sister for what she did.
She dropped it. Just carelessly dropped it.
Now it's gone. Dead.
Mum says to get over it.
How can I? Only got 'im last week.
It was everywhere, just red everywhere.
I remember breaking down in a fit of tears.
I knew it had to go sometime,
But not then, not like that.
Yet my sister just didn't care.
She handled him far too roughly.
It will always have a special place in my heart.
My first bottle of Heinz ketchup.

Naomi Gabriel (14)
Wakefield Girls' High School

Be cause It All Flows Back Around . . .

I shout myself raw in mutual vein.
Those guitar-plucked pulses vibrate the walls.
Like those new formed feet once fought the fleshy womb.
We've fought worse battles since then.
I see those feet now. Size sixes in those clumsy boots
And watch as she trudges and tramples her troubles to dust.

It rose to the surface so fast.
As her heel rose and her hair rinsed plum.
My earring lost, and found. Not in her ear.
A dog left without a collar.
Rapid as breath Kylie changed to Robbie,
Then Robbie got old and was replaced by strangers, wearing masks.

But it's my eyes I see through the holes in her mask.
And it's my flesh behind the make-up.
And Robert Plant is not so far from Kurt Cobain.
The lines may have changed, but I've walked them too.
Maybe it's true, and the song remains the same.

Amy Pond (17)
Wakefield Girls' High School

Shark! (Haiku)

The white shark attacks,
Tearing your delicate skin.
There is no escape.

Sally-Ann Holroyd (11)
Wakefield Girls' High School

My Emblem Of Purity

On unicorn with coat so white
Galloping gracefully through the night
Your divine chastity is such
Tamed only by a virgin's touch
Your horn is like a treasured charm
It keeps you safe and free from harm

Oh unicorn with coat so white
When cornered you would nobly fight
You can't be hurt by pain or love
Your soul is free just like a dove
Your silky mane flows in the wind
Your blood is sought by those who've sinned

Oh unicorn with coat so white
Galloping gracefully through the night
My imagination has run its course
For you are but a lonely horse.

Abbey Sykes (15)
Wakefield Girls' High School

Siberian Tiger

Prowling in the night
White fur glistening in the moon
Roaring and searching

The chill of the wind
Dew shimmering on the grass
Bare trees stand alone

Empty, dark and scarce
Full of the twinkling stars
Lifeless is the place.

Hannah Perry (11)
Wakefield Girls' High School

I Wonder If My Children's Children . . .

I wonder if my children's children
Will grow up in a world with stars?
Will the Earth have spun out of orbit?
Will we all be living on Mars?

Will hippos rule the planet?
Will we all have to speak in French?
Will there still be raindrops
Dripping on the garden bench?

Will there still be tigers
Prowling through the night?
Will there still be TV?
Will we still have rights?

All I know is this;
I shan't be standing there, gazing.
It'll be my children's children's problem,
For I'll be pushing up daisies.

Margaret Browning (13)
Wakefield Girls' High School

The 'Jungle' And The Garden

Acres of jungle lie ahead!
Metres of grass lie ahead.
I fight my way through!
I walk over to the swing.
A snake! An elephant!
A worm! A snail!
The tall trees that dominate the sky!
The green grass dominates the ground.
I clamber over something large and pink!
Something's tickling my bare feet - it's an ant!

Rachael Honeyman (11)
Wakefield Girls' High School

Imagination

I left the world
This hallowed eve
I left it in the
Murky breeze
I saw the spirits
Of the dead
Woken from their
Silent bed
I walked across
The seventh land
I walked there
With an open hand
I thought of all
The things I'd miss
I thought of life
Its dying kiss
I contemplated just today
What I'd do if I couldn't say . . .
I wondered
In fear
What life would be
Without imagination
This vast
Growing
Tree . . .

Rebecca Frith (11)
Wakefield Girls' High School

If Only . . .

If only people would think,
Then mess and misunderstandings would never even exist.
If only weapons were not invented,
Then lives would not be dead.

If only everyone treated each other the same,
Then colour, religion, height and weight would not matter
                                    in a great person.
If only peace was always permanent,
Then our minds would be put at rest.

If only people would listen,
Then the important comments would not be misheard.
If only criticism was not said,
Then hearts would not be hurt.

If only competitiveness was not so determined,
Then competitions would be fun.
If only time machines really existed,
Then all the wrong doings could be put right.

If only . . .

Samantha Wynn (12)
Wakefield Girls' High School

The Pond

Once a world of flowing life,
A fountain of coloured ribbons dancing.
When the wind blew, the reeds swayed silently,
Like the grass as a cat stalks.
A placid place of calm and rest.
A place to have a quiet sneeze in the gentle sun.
Now it's no longer that, but now a concrete prison.
The fish won't dance and the reeds won't sway.
A place of quiet but in a different way.
Just a desert of emptiness,
For the creatures of the pond.
Memories, not smiles.

Stephanie Chui (12)
Wakefield Girls' High School

Winter

It's cold, I shiver
My nose turns rosy-red
My jaw hangs open
And my hat goes over

My head, my ears
I'm frozen to the ground
I'll just stand still
And hang there like an

Icicle, a snowflake
Both falling to the ground
Then someone comes and breaks me
Because with friends they play

On sleighs, with wellies
Running all around
Decorating Christmas trees
And then their mums shout

Them in.

Laura Everett (11)
Wakefield Girls' High School

Shadowed - Haiku Verses

I wander the streets,
Carefully checking around,
Looking behind me.

I heard footsteps near,
Crunching in the fallen leaves,
I swivelled around.

There was a shadow,
A shadow in the darkness,
Moving through the dark.

Shadows are scary,
What do you think?

Amy Barrick (12)
Wakefield Girls' High School

Boredom

Boredom is so boring.
It's just waiting . . . waiting . . . waiting
For something, anything, to happen.
No one dare break the ear-splitting silence,
Not a cough or a sneeze to be heard.
I get an urge to jump up and scream out loud,
But I don't.
There are only so many times you can twiddle your thumbs,
And you can't tap your toes forever.
The eyes in sockets roll like bowling balls,
Re-reading everything over and over again.
Frequent trips to the loo are made,
Just for something to do.
And then there's the business of
'Just going for a breath of fresh air'
Yes - boredom is really very boring.

Elizabeth Brown (12)
Wakefield Girls' High School

The Guitar

Sat quietly in the room
No one watching
No one hearing
No one knowing
She picks up the case - unzips
Pulls out the instrument
Her fingers tenderly touch the strings
She pulls

Music fills the silent air
One long note
Joyous and yet sorrowful
Then as it started it stopped
The harmony was broken
Softly again, again, again
Strum, strum, strum.

Victoria Finan (12)
Wakefield Girls' High School

Alone

She sits alone upon the tear-stained ground,
Her hands home and shelter her scrawny, gaunt face.
The vast, unwelcoming room engulfs her in its dark depression,
Tears stream down her cheeks as if they're running a deplorable race.

She squats in a house but it's not a home,
A gust of wind wanders through the room like a forgotten
                                        spirit whistling.
Wanting to be noticed.
She owns no credentials, no possessions to her name,
She bothers no one yet for everything that happens,
                        she's homeless so she's to blame.

The stares, the looks, the snide comments she witnesses as
                                she hobbles through the street,
Looking for some work, a job to pass the never-ending day.
She lives a nightmare over and over in her mind,
Tomorrow is deeply dreaded, she sees no glimmer of hope,
                                no light, not even a ray.

She looms over a small candle trying desperately to feel the heat,
Her eyes close willingly and she falls into a deep dream of
                                unknown happiness.
Her time has come to go into a better life, her eyes are shut,
                        her skin is pale, her heart, it does not beat.
She is alone no more.

Bethan Crossley (12)
Wakefield Girls' High School

But Then You Came

It's dark where I live,
It's cold and it's gloomy,
I had nothing to look forward to,
Nothing to laugh about,
Nothing to call mine.
I used to sit there hungry,
Lonely, tired and sad,
My brothers and sisters would go to work,
But I couldn't; I was too young.
No one could hear my restless cries,
My longings, my pleas, my tears.
But then you came.
Like an angel from above.
You were a dream, a miracle, a treasure chest
Even though you were just a shoebox.
But to me, you were a prized possession.
As a gold medal is to an athlete.
As a blanket to a child.
As a baby to its mother.
I don't know where you came from,
Or why you came
But you put a smile on my face.
You really changed my life.

Nikhita Bhandari (12)
Wakefield Girls' High School

The Railway

White steam gushing out of my funnel,
My wheels spinning along the track,
All my sacks with mail in the back,
So heavy to haul up the hills.

I hear the whistling of the station master,
And my wheels chugging along,
Looking out of my window to see . . .
I'm in a deep, dark, dark tunnel.

I see the birds fluttering by,
And the woolly sheep on the green, grassy meadows,
I hear the cows mooing in the fields,
And the trees swaying from side to side.

I arrive at Glasgow's busy, busy station,
All the chit, chit, chatter-chatter I hear,
The noises are so very, very clear,
Everyone so excited to board the train.

Business men and women in their formal suits,
Little children racing about trying to find their parents,
Schoolgirls in smart uniforms all waiting to leave for school,
The odd couple in a corner, snogging for evermore.

I bring the mail to the people and let the passengers enjoy
their destination,
When my train is light-weighted,
I start my engine so it is up and running,
Then I slowly disappear.

Reena Patel (13)
Wakefield Girls' High School

The Match

Our uniformed organisation stands proud and assumes
the position for the start of play.
The enemy approaches, goal defence sidles up against me, a tank,
the driving force of the opposition.
Suddenly I feel small and wounded.
And then it begins.
Our front line troops grapple for the ball as the back-up forces
defend rival territory;
a frenzy of feet down the wing causes a sandstorm,
obscuring our vision.
Our only equipment, our only supplies are our limbs - both teams
sneakily try underhand methods to deviously seal victory.
But all in vain for our visitors, our secret weapon prepares
to fire the bomb into the net.
It explodes right on target; my shot is greeted by rapturous cheering
to mirror the missile's effect.
However the casualties are piling up.
Half-time, and our rations are delivered.
How good those oranges taste!
More allies and reinforcements are sent from our sideline base
onto the battlefield, as many limp away injured.
Two, three, four goals we concede, but still our brave soldiers fight
on to equalise and then take the lead - I lose track of the tally.
The sergeant barks orders nearby; the conflict is far from over yet.
Time is running out and our platoon is surrendering, will we triumph?
A blast of inspiration from our defence gives us the will to succeed,
a new energy.
We fire the projectile down the court. I catch it in the shooting circle.
Twenty seconds left, our last chance to defeat them . . .
can I convert this crucial shot into a goal?
I can.
The final whistle sounds, we emerge victorious! I did it!

The battle is won.

Zoë Proud (13)
Wakefield Girls' High School

Night Mare

Swift as an eagle, it bounds down the moor
Crunching cobs of crisp corn every now and then
Nuzzling strangers in return for a stroke
Tossing its mane majestically in joy.

It waits and gazes intently at the surroundings
Its eyes as wide as marbles in the sun
Glittering white teeth and neatly shaven fur
Tail as straight and wispy as one of a mouse.

The beautiful silhouette of the beast
Is visible in the dark, gloomy sky
Radiant, bright skin stands out clearly in the night
Elegant leaps and strides it takes
The marvellous scene it makes.

Suddenly it freezes and looks aghast
A speck of light filters in through the sky
The beautiful creature stands astounded at the sight
The charm and the body of the beast begin to fade.

It is a night mare
Its time has passed away
It is time for it to rest
It is time for dawn to rise.

Kiruthika Rajeswaran (11)
Wakefield Girls' High School

Passenger

Jolt.
Passively, we move,
Bodies reluctant to resist.
Jolt.
A woman's voice,
At exactly the right RP pitch,
Soars along the bus.
Jolt.
Neon letters
Glide like oil
Over the smooth black sign.
Destination: end of the line.
Jolt.
Yellow poles
Leer
At the other drab furnishings.
Grab
From behind, a hand
Seizes the pole.
Another passenger slips
Into the night outside.
Jolt.
The thick winter air
Licks the window.
Move into the aisle;
False electric comfort.
Jolt.
Realisation;
Another jolt will mean
Me
Sliding off the bus,
Into whatever waits outside.
Jolt.

Hannah Walker Gore (15)
Wakefield Girls' High School

The Journey

Yesterday I found something,
It was coloured blue and green
And on the side in big, black letters,
Were the words 'Time Machine'.
I picked it up and turned it round and shook it very hard,
And as I did, out flew instructions on a piece of card.
Press the button, blink one eye, count to ten in Greek,
Hop on one leg, hold on tight and say the days of the week.
A sudden noise, and a flashing sound, my world was torn apart.
And there I was, sat on a horse, beside Richard the Lionheart.
I couldn't stay, I had to fly, I had to meet the Queen,
Victoria said, 'I'm not amused and where on earth have you been?'
I didn't have time to answer; my head was in a spin
And suddenly I was talking magic with the wizard, Merlin.
I sang with Elvis Presley, helped Shakespeare write a play,
Had a chat with Einstein and saw Columbus on his way,
The time machine was flashing, its energy getting low.
I better get a move on, before the fuses blow!
My brain is in confusion, was it all a dream?
But I can remember all the people I met,
And all the places I had seen . . .

Rachael Dyer   (13)
Wakefield Girls' High School

My Cry

A snowflake plunders down my skin,
It reveals the sadness that lies within,
Yet crying isn't an awful sin,
But no one hears me cry.

A river now trickles down my cheek,
I'm so upset I cannot speak,
And happiness I try to seek,
But no one hears me cry.

And now the river turns into a flood,
It melts my smile and chills my blood,
And now a teardrop lands with a thud,
Will someone hear me cry?

New tears come to replace the old,
Now I am lonely and now I am cold,
And I wish someone soon were told,
That no one's heard my cry.

And I face the truth now with a sigh,
That if no one passes by,
That grieving will come with me till I die,
Because no one heard my cry.

Sally Greenwood (11)
Wakefield Girls' High School

Grandma Grice

*(Dedicated to my great grandma who unfortunately
passed away on the 4th October 2003)*

My grandma Grice had a great life,
At a very young age she became a wife.
She and her husband would dance all night,
They would in dark or in light.

Christine and Ruth were their daughters,
And as a family they loved to walk round waters.
For a holiday they'd go to Blackpool,
Just to see the laughing fool.

Her children left, so she retired,
Her new skill, watercolours, was very admired.
Soon she got some delightful grandkids,
And later on, even some great grandkids.

All of a sudden her husband, Grandad Grice, died,
So then her children became her guide.
She lived on for a few more years,
And there were still plenty of cheers.

In October 2003 we said goodbye to Grandma Grice.
As a great grandma she was very, very nice.

Maria Câmara Brook (11)
Wakefield Girls' High School

Bang!

A cold, hard stare,
A devil's stare.
The two enemies,
Shooting evil looks at each other.
Their mouths dry, their palms sweaty.
The atmosphere gets tenser every second.
The two enemies take a look back at their beloved families.
Then turn and take ten manly steps.
With each step their stomachs turn.
1, 2, 3,
The peasant leads.
4, 5, 6,
The king is catching up.
7, 8, 9,
They're neck and neck.
10!
Bang!
The peasant ducks and misses the bullet flying towards him.
The king falls with a scream.
Dead
So easily, so quickly. Too quick!

Alexandra Calvert (11)
Wakefield Girls' High School